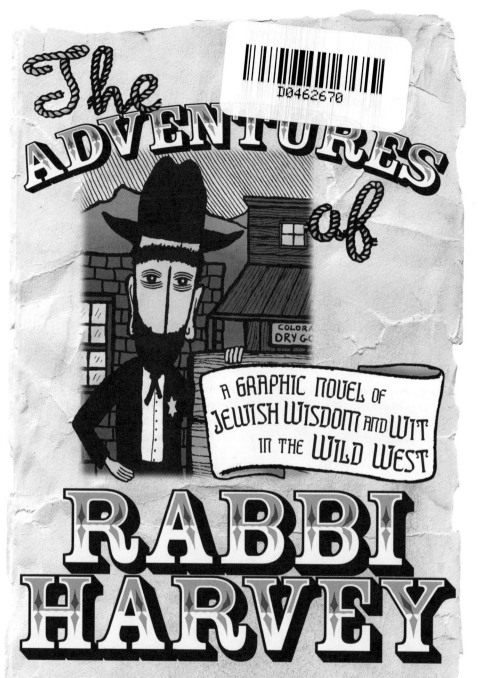

The ADVENTURES of

A GRAPHIC NOVEL OF JEWISH WISDOM AND WIT IN THE WILD WEST

RABBI HARVEY

STEVE SHEINKIN

For People of All Faiths, All Backgrounds

JEWISH LIGHTS Publishing
Woodstock, Vermont
www.jewishlights.com

The Adventures of Rabbi Harvey:
A Graphic Novel of Jewish Wisdom and Wit in the Wild West

2016 Third Printing

For information regarding permission to reprint material from this book, please mail or fax your request in writing to Jewish Lights Publishing, Permissions Department, at the address / fax number listed below, or email your request to permissions@jewishlights.com.

© 2006 by Stephen Sheinkin

Library of Congress Cataloging-in-Publication Data
Sheinkin, Steve.
  The adventures of Rabbi Harvey : a graphic novel of Jewish wisdom and wit in the Wild West / Steve Sheinkin.
    p. cm.
  ISBN-13: 978-1-58023-310-1
  ISBN-10: 1-58023-310-4
  1. Graphic novels. I. Title.

PN6727.S495A38 2006
  741.5—dc22
                                    2006045794

10 9 8 7 6 5 4 3

Cover design: Sara Dismukes

Manufactured in the United States of America

For People of All Faiths, All Backgrounds
Published by Jewish Lights Publishing
A Division of LongHill Partners, Inc.
Sunset Farm Offices, Route 4, P.O. Box 237
Woodstock, VT 05091
Tel: (802) 457-4000   Fax: (802) 457-4004
www.jewishlights.com

CONTENTS

The Rabbi Harvey Series
Written and Illustrated by Steve Sheinkin

The Adventures of Rabbi Harvey
A Graphic Novel of Jewish Wisdom and Wit in the Wild West

Rabbi Harvey Rides Again
A Graphic Novel of Jewish Folktales Let Loose in the Wild West

Rabbi Harvey vs. the Wisdom Kid
A Graphic Novel of Dueling Jewish Folktales in the Wild West

INTRODUCTION

When I was a kid I had two books that fell apart because I read them so often: *101 Jewish Stories* and a collection of Wild West adventures. I saw no deep connection between these favorites—they were just books of fantastic stories, with odd characters you could follow around and hang out with after the sentences ended.

Many years later I began writing a comic about a rabbi named Harvey, in which tales of Jewish wisdom came to life on the streets of the western frontier. This seemed perfectly normal to me. It was only as I explained the idea to friends that I realized I was describing an unusual combination of elements. That's when I looked for a logical link. And it was pretty easy to find.

I have never actually lived in a *shtetl* in Eastern Europe or a frontier town in the Rocky Mountains. But I feel a personal connection, a tugging attraction, to both places—or at least to some mythical version of both places. I think this is because, as an American Jew, I have the great fortune to have been born with a bond to both Jewish and American traditions and folklore. So the ingredients of Jewish and American stories were mixed in my head long before I began mixing them in a comic.

What I have tried to do in *The Adventures of Rabbi Harvey* is collect stories and small gems from a variety of sources: classic Jewish folktales; Hasidic legends from the likes of the Baal Shem Tov, Rebbe Nachman of Breslov, and Zusya of Anipol; and Talmudic teachings, like those found in *Pirke Avot*, the Ethics of the Sages. The book's action is set in the fictional town of Elk Spring, high in the mountains of Colorado. The graphic novel format felt right because it allowed me to tell these stories the way I always imagined them. And to add plenty of gags.

The book's hero, Rabbi Harvey, protects his town and delivers justice wielding only the weapons of wisdom, kindness, and humor. He's part old world rabbi, part western sheriff. He's also part David, my father. My father gave me that first book of Jewish stories. And this book is for him.

MEET RABBI HARVEY

Near the town of Elk Spring, Colorado, high in the Rocky Mountains, there lived a man named Nathan. He was a candle maker. But what he really loved to do was read. He would have sat and read for a living, but no one would pay him to do it.

So Nathan worked all day, then read at night by the light of his candles.

Nathan's candle workshop was right behind his house.

Maybe today I'll make yellow ...

Here he is working with Ruth, his wife. She usually joined him in the workshop as soon as their two sons left for school.

And when the boys came home, Nathan took a break to read with them.

There was once a very tiny king....

... and on top of candle making, I'm sort of an expert on ancient Rome.

Ask me anything.

I'm sorry sir, I just don't have any work for you.

You might talk to Rabbi Harvey.

How could he help?

I don't know, but they say he gives the best advice this side of the Mississippi.

The baker was right. Rabbi Harvey was famous throughout the West for his wisdom and kindness. People traveled over mountains to see him. So Nathan decided to speak to the Rabbi.

The Rabbi was in his office doing a little sweeping.

Oh, I'm bound ♫ to follow the longhorn cows, until I git ♫ too old....

There was a knock on the door.

Hello, Rabbi. I'm Nathan the candle maker. I've come for some advice.

Okay, but I know very little about candles.

Nathan told his story to Rabbi Harvey. He was a little nervous, though, and it took him a very long time to get to the point.

... and then for my tenth birthday I got a rock polisher ...

I see.

The Rabbi interrupted.

Quick— name the twelve sons of Jacob.

Reuben, Simeon, Levi, Judah, Issacher, Zebulun, Dan, Naphtali, Gad, Asher, Joseph, Benjamin.

Nice. I can never remember Dan. At any rate, I know of a job teaching children.

Rabbi: But the job is in a town far from here.

Nathan: How far?

Rabbi: Utah.

Nathan: That's far.

Rabbi: It's not close.

But Nathan's family needed the money. So the next morning, he woke up early and started out for Utah.

So that weekend, Nathan went to the market. He hoped to find a traveling merchant who was on his way to Colorado.

Buy this!

No, buy this!

Big deals!

Why walk around in rags, friends? Come have a look in my famous Fashion Wagon!

Good day, sir. Tell me, will you be traveling to the town of Elk Spring, Colorado, any time soon?

Might be, might be. Say, that hat looks like it was run over by my Fashion Wagon. Let me show you some of the latest styles from back East.

No thank you, sir. But maybe you could take this money to my wife?

Rather not. No time.

Come see the Fashion Wagon!

What next?

Can we Dad?

Sir, I must have your help. If you will only take this small bag of coins to my wife, you can give her as much of the money as you want.

As much as I want? Am I crazy or is there a nice chance for profit here?

Nathan put the unusual deal into writing.

When do I get to see the Fashion Wagon?

FASHION WAGON

The merchant took the bag of silver dollars and headed east on the mountain road to Colorado.

There was one little goat, one very little goat, that my father bought for two zuzim....

He arrived at Nathan's house the following week.

KNOCK! KNOCK!

Then came a cat, and ate the goat....

The merchant came in and walked to the table. Ruth followed. The merchant took a single coin from the sack. He threw it on the table. It lay there all alone.

Ruth read the note that Nathan had written. And she did not understand how her husband could have made such a foolish deal.

But Ruth was almost positive that her husband was not an idiot. She insisted that they go to Rabbi Harvey for a judgment. They would let him decide who should keep the one hundred silver dollars. The merchant agreed, feeling the law was clearly on his side. They walked to town without talking.

Ruth knocked on the Rabbi's door and they waited.

RABBI ★

PLEASE KNOCK

I hope that's the traveling trout salesman.

Rabbi Harvey agreed to hear the case. He asked Ruth and the merchant to present their arguments at the same time. He was so used to hearing disputes that he could easily listen to two people talk at once.

Can you believe that, Rabbi?

So you can see how I would feel, Rabbi.

Amazing. Go on, please.

Of course. Very interesting.

When Ruth and the merchant finished talking, the Rabbi turned to the merchant, looked him in the eye, and said:

And you're sure you can give this woman only one dollar?

That's up to me, isn't it?

So it would seem. Let's see that note.

The Rabbi studied Nathan's note.

Ah, candle maker.... I see your game.

Then the Rabbi turned to Ruth.

Your husband is a very clever man.

You think so?

Watch this.

Tell me again, merchant. Exactly how much of this money do you want?

Ninety-nine dollars, Rabbi. Two nines.

Very well, then. Here is my decision. But wait, there's not enough room on the page.

There was a knock on the door.

Who is it?

Trout man!

Come in!

Rabbi Harvey offered to cook dinner for his guests. Ruth said she had to get back home to her children, but the merchant accepted the invite. The Rabbi bought two rainbow trout and prepared them in a wine and butter sauce. All through dinner, the merchant attempted to sell Harvey a new suit.

Seriously, Harv. I'd love to see you in one of my new Italian three-pieces. Why, you'd be the sharpest-looking rabbi in five counties!

Come on, Harv, finish up your fish and we'll step out to the Fashion Wagon. Wait till you see the stuff I just got from my man in New York. You will love it!

It's a hard job, being the Rabbi.

RABBI HARVEY: BEARDED CHICKEN

There was once a boy named Asher. He was ten years old. He thought he was a chicken. He lived under the kitchen table.

Bock, bock. I'm a talking chicken.

He ate only bread crumbs. He would not wear clothes. He refused to go to school.

Why should a chicken have to learn history?

Asher's parents were concerned. They did not like the idea of having a chicken for a son.

How about a piece of steak, Asher?

I don't eat my friends.

They were always embarrassed when people came to visit.

Hal, is that your boy under the table?

Yeah, he was doing his homework and he dropped his pencil.

I see. But that doesn't explain why he pecked at my toe when I said hello to him.

Come outside and look at my new barn.

Many weeks went by. Asher continued to insist that he was a chicken. His parents finally began to lose patience with their boy.

Look, Asher, are you coming out from under the table or not?

Cluck.

Cluck!

We'll give you five more minutes, then we're putting you outside.

Five minutes later:

Cluck, cluck.

Rabbi Harvey heard about the unusual boy. He decided to see if there was anything he could do to help.

I once knew a man who thought he was a pine tree ...

He was very old, though.

Greetings, Hal. Nice barn.

Thanks, Rabbi.

Tell me, is it true your son believes he is a chicken?

No, Rabbi! What a ridiculous question!

I just saw him. He was nude and eating corn from the ground.

Oh. Yeah, that's him.

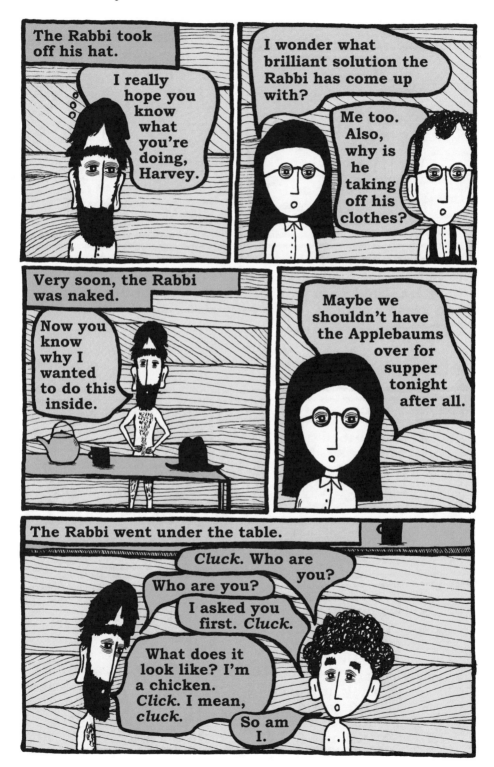

That's obvious. Anyone can see that you're a chicken.

They can?

Sure.

Listen, you don't mind if I live here with you, do you?

Cluck. I guess not.

Cluck.

So Asher and the Rabbi, both chickens, lived together under the kitchen table. For breakfast and lunch, they ate dried corn from the floor. For dinner, they had bread crumbs.

They got along quite well.

What bread do you feel makes the best crumbs?

Rye.

I like pumpernickel.

They sang chicken songs.

No there never was a chicken like Asher ♫ the chicken!

Well, now we have two chickens.

I wouldn't mind so much if they at least laid an egg now and then.

At this point, it wouldn't surprise me.

Asher found this reasoning to be logical. He put on his shirt.

Bock bock.

So tell me, do you feel like any less of a chicken now?

No.

Me neither.

Two more days passed.

... then Noah sent forth a dove from the ark, to see if the earth was still under water.

He should have sent a chicken.

I'm going to town, Hal. What do we need?

A new barrel of chicken feed.

Besides that.

I've been thinking again, Asher. The thing is, I really feel like putting my pants on. But I still want to be a chicken. What should I do?

Asher thought for a minute.

I'm not sure. Why don't we both put on our pants and see how we feel?

Asher's father brought their pants. They put them on. They also put on socks and shoes, just to see how they felt.

What do you think?

Not bad.

And the best part is, I'm just as much of a chicken as ever!

We both are!

They broke into song.

He's Harvey, Harvey, hero to all bearded chickens! ♪

Another day went by. After lunch, Asher and the Rabbi had a little talk.

I'm not really sure.

Something has been troubling me, Asher.

What?

It's just ... how come chickens have to live under a table?

It seems to me a chicken should be able to stand up and walk around. A chicken should be able to do anything he wants.

But the Rabbi loved baseball and he really wanted to play. Asher agreed to give it a try.

And he actually hit the ball.

But not too far.

They put the Rabbi out in right field, where he made a brilliant running catch on a long fly ball.

The game went on for hours. It finally ended in the bottom of the thirteenth on a long homer over the post office. Asher played fairly well. Each time up, he hit the ball a tiny bit farther. The Rabbi, on the other hand, struggled with the bat. Let's face it, he struck out six times.

You should play with us more often, Asher.

Thanks.

You can play with us too, Rabbi. I guess.

Thanks.

But you'll probably be too busy.

The Rabbi suggested they get some lunch at Sara's Cafe.

I hope this is alright. I mean, chickens can eat in restaurants if they want, can't they?

Sure. And you shouldn't be ashamed of being a chicken, but ...

I don't feel like being a chicken anymore.

I see.... Well, it's no fun being the only talking chicken in town. Maybe I'll just go back to being a regular rabbi.

We can still be friends, can't we?

Sure. Just look at us! A boy and a rabbi, enjoying a little lunch together!

Sara came to the table.

Our special today is one of your favorites, Rabbi. Fried chicken in a basket!

I'll have the pancakes.

THE JUICE PRINCESS

Imagine you were Abraham, and God told you to sacrifice your beloved son. What would you do?

Pretend to be too busy?

Interesting.

Every Monday afternoon, Rabbi Harvey tutored Lisa in Hebrew and Bible studies. Lisa was the daughter of Julius Jaffa, a very wealthy orchard owner and juice maker. Julius called himself "The Juice King of the Rockies." He called his daughter "The Juice Princess."

Now I have a question for you, Rabbi.

Yes?

You're such a wise man, but....

You have to admit, you're kind of funny-looking, I mean, not very handsome. Isn't it a shame that so much knowledge is kept in such a ... well ... ugly head?

Perhaps you are right.

I am?

Certainly.

I'm curious. What type of vessels does your father store his own juice in?

Those big clay jugs, of course. Haven't you seen them at the store?

Sure. I go through a gallon of apple-grape every week.

But your father is the Juice KING! Shouldn't his own juice be kept in something more special than clay jugs?

Lisa agreed. As soon as she got home, she poured all of her father's own personal juice into pitchers and bowls of gold.

APPLES

Wait until Father sees what I have done!

Now, have you ever tried keeping juice in an open metal container? If you have, then you probably know what Lisa didn't—that it will quickly become smelly and rotten.

That evening, Mr. Julius Jaffa sat down to dinner.

I'm ready for dinner, Lisa! Tonight I think I'll have juice!

Mr. Jaffa didn't believe in eating food.

Coming right up, Papa!

The finest juice from the finest vessel!

Lisa watched.

Julius drank.

Lisa ducked.

But your father is the Juice KING! Shouldn't his juice be kept in some...

You ruined my juice!!!

The next time they met, Lisa told the Rabbi all about what happened.

To punish me, he made me drink five cups of rotten orange juice.

That hurts.

I told him it was your idea. And he said that storing juice in golden vessels was very foolish.

Yes, I suppose your father is right.

RABBI HARVEY: HUMAN SCALE

One day, a reporter from Denver came to Elk Spring to do a story about Rabbi Harvey. The reporter nicknamed Harvey "The Human Scale." The name was based on Harvey's famous ability to listen to two sides of any dispute, weigh the evidence, and come up with a fair judgment.

The photographer had Harvey pose like a scale.

I feel like a fool.

Perfect, Harv! Hold still for one more!

The story came out later that month.

I sure hope my father doesn't see this ...

And while the article was certainly silly, it got one thing right: Rabbi Harvey really *was* an expert at making fair judgments.

As he told the reporter:

People think I have some kind of special ability ...

I don't.

But please don't tell anyone. You see, sometimes it really helps that people think I'm smart.

For instance, I remember one time when three businessmen came to see me. They owned a lumber mill together down on Black Bear River. Money was missing from their safe and everyone knew one of them must have taken it. But when confronted, each man denied the theft.

Wasn't me.

Wasn't me.

Wasn't me.

Gentlemen, one of you is lying to me.

Not me.

It's very foolish to lie to me, gentlemen. As you know, I can always tell when someone is not being truthful.

Like me right now, for example.

The men were silent.

And not only do I know when someone is lying, I sometimes have visions as well. They just come to me. Right now I am seeing the barn of the guilty man—he knows who he is. It appears to me that his house is about to catch fire.

Yes, yes, I see it quite clearly. There is a candle, there is a cow ...

Hmm, how did the cow get into the kitchen? Ah, I see, the door was left open ... she is walking toward the candle ... she is going to knock it over ... no, she missed it, the house is safe! But wait, I spoke too soon, the cow is coming back....

Gentlemen, if you will excuse me for a moment.

The man ran out.

I've always hated that cow.

Rabbi, could you check your vision again and see if our money is burning up?

The money is safe.

Or sometimes I can just tell right away who is lying. In such cases, I try to solve the problem without humiliating anyone in public.

The Reporter

Give me an example, Harv.

There was the time Mr. Katz lost his wallet. He's a rich man, and always keeps a lot of money on him.

The wallet was found by Will Brown, the wheel maker.

Look what I found, son! A wallet with two hundred dollars!

Dad, everyone knows that Old Man Katz lost his wallet yesterday and if you find it you have to give it back.

What if I keep it?

How much did you say there was?

Two hundred.

Sweet *Bubbe!* Still, you have to return it.

I knew you would say that.

Sorry, pop.

I guess you're right, son. But two hundred dollars sure would come in handy....

Will decided to bring the money back and hope for a small reward.

With two hundred dollars I could ... well, let's not even think about it.

He knocked on Mr. Katz's door.

I believe this belongs to you?

Yes.

Mr. Katz counted the money. He chuckled to himself.

What a fool this guy is! He actually returns a wallet full of cash! No one that stupid deserves a reward.

Mr. Katz decided to have some fun with the wheel maker.

There's only two hundred dollars in here. It had three hundred when I lost it.

I know your game, pal. You figured I'd be so glad to get my wallet back, I wouldn't mind the missing hundred.

No, I ...

Or do you take me for a senile old fool who forgot how to count?

Hold on, are you accusing me of stealing?

I certainly am. And you can add "not being too bright" to the list of charges.

The men came to me for a judgment. Each man presented his case.

I could judge this in my sleep.

He stole a hundred. Let *that* be his reward.

Let me get this clear. How much money was in the wallet you lost?

Three hundred dollars.

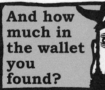

And how much in the wallet you found?

Two hundred, Rabbi.

Very well. You are both honorable men and would not lie to me. Which leaves only one possibility.

The wallet Will Brown found was not Mr. Katz's wallet. You see, Mr. Katz's wallet contained three hundred dollars. And Mr. Brown found a wallet with only two hundred. Clearly, we have two different wallets here.

The law in such cases is very clear. No one claimed the wallet with two hundred dollars, so it goes back to its finder, Will Brown. Congratulations on your good fortune, Mr. Brown.

Thanks, Rabbi.

As for you, Mr. Katz, your luck is not as good. But we will keep an eye out for your wallet.

I deserved that.

Thanks, Rabbi.

Great story, Harv, just super. Boy, you and wisdom go together like ham and cheese.

I'll have to take your word for it.

Give me one more story, Harv. And make it a humorous one. My readers love to have a good laugh.

Haven't all my stories been humorous?

Okay, I'll try.

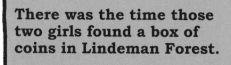

There was the time those two girls found a box of coins in Lindeman Forest.

Look at me! I'm on the tallest branch in the world!

Judy

Hey, what's that thing down there?

Where?

Jane

Jane looked down. There was a box.

Look what I found!

The box was filled with nickels.

Look at them all!

We're rich!

The girls spilled the coins onto the ground. There was over twenty dollars.

Let's split it up.

Okay. Wait, I have even a better idea.

We don't want people asking a lot of annoying questions about how we got so much money.

So we should each take ten cents now and leave the rest hidden. And we can come get a little bit every day.

You're so smart, Jane.

They hid the box in an old oak tree.

That night Jane went for a walk. Guess why.

This is interesting, Harv, don't get me wrong. But where are the laughs?

Stick with me.

The girls came to see me.

And they told me their story.

I have a pretty good idea of what happened here. But I can't resist making a little game of it.

Tell me this, girls. Was there no one else in the woods? No one who might have witnessed the theft of the money?

No, Rabbi.

Not that we saw.

Then there is only one option I can think of. We will have to ask the only witness to the crime—the tree. Naturally, the tree will have seen who took the money. And trees, oaks especially, are well known for their honesty.

That could be a problem.

The girls seemed to doubt my theory about oak trees. But I insisted that it was the only way to solve the mystery. I set the trial for ten the next morning. Jane ran home and made a very strange request of her father. He's a shoemaker, by the way.

You want me to do *what*?

It's a game! You hide in a hollow tree, and if anyone talks to you, you just say, "Judy took the money."

You know I'd do anything for you, Jane, but ... I have ten pair of boots to re-sole by noon tomorrow.

Please, Daddy?

How long would I have to be in the tree?

The next morning I walked through Lindeman Forest toward the hollow tree.

At the foot on yon mountain, where the fountain doth flow, Where the birds circle high, where the soft wind doth blow, There lived a fair maiden, she's the one I adore,

She's the one I will marry, on the Red River shore. I asked her father to give her hand to me. "No sir, she shan't marry no cowboy," said he....

By the time I got to the tree, a small crowd had already gathered.

And admit it, Harv, you love to work in front of a crowd.

Perhaps. I only wish so many people showed up in temple.

Are both children here?

Yes, Rabbi.

Right here, Rabbi.

Good. Now let's get started.

I stepped up to the hollow tree. I knocked.

Okay, tree. Tell us what you saw. Don't be shy.

I realize the Rabbi is a little bit different ... but this is just plain old weird.

The tree did not answer my question. Jane began to cough loudly.

cough! cough!

She also kicked the tree three times.

Finally, the tree spoke.

Sorry, could you repeat the question?

I wasn't expecting the tree to speak such good English.

We were all just standing here and wondering ... did you happen to see who took the box of coins from the hole in your trunk?

Judy took the money.

I then turned to the tree.

As for you, tree, you saw this crime and did nothing to stop it. In fact, you did not even bother to report it. It is almost as if you played a part in the crime yourself.

But—

No buts.

We must make an example of this tree. If only for the sake of the young trees.

I rule that you should be burned down right now.

That's a bit harsh.

Sorry, my judgment is final.

Someone bring me a match!

Wait a minute! Don't light that match!

A sound came from inside the tree. Soon, a pair of shoes appeared, followed by two legs.

Do you see feet sticking out of me?

Yes.

Please pull them.

THERE'S A NEW RABBI IN TOWN

Many years ago, before the arrival of Rabbi Harvey, the town of Elk Spring, Colorado, was ruled by a small band of ruthless outlaws (pictured below). The band was led by a man named Milton "Big Milt" Wasserman. Big Milt claimed to be the smartest, toughest guy in the West. And maybe he was.

You better believe it.

Daniel "The Lion" Levy

"Big Milt" Wasserman

Moses "Matzah Man" Goldwater

Big Milt and his men held the whole town in their hands.

It's tax time again, Mr. Vincent. My records show that you owe us one dollar.

Here you are, sir.

Good boy.

The store owners were helpless.

Give me ten pounds of every kind of food you have. And two new suits. And four hats. And put it on my tab.

And when will you be paying that tab, if I may ask?

The fifth of never.

Sounds fair.

Even the restaurant was unsafe.

Buuuuuuuurrrrrrrrppp! Three more matzah pot pies! And more coffee!

It was at this time that young Rabbi Harvey finished his studies in New York City. He had always dreamed of seeing the West, so he bought a train ticket to Denver. He began looking for work in the area, but rabbi jobs were scarce.

I could always go back to my old job at the pickle factory.

At least then I ate well. If you can call two pounds of pickles a day eating well.

But Harvey refused to give up. He visited hundreds of towns.

Are you sure you can't use me? I would be willing to consider a part-time position.

It's a very hard field to break into, son. We rabbis all live so long, there are never any openings.

Harvey was tired and hungry when he came to the town of Elk Spring.

Should I even bother?

Harvey walked through the deserted streets of downtown Elk Spring. People were afraid to go outside. But Harvey didn't know this.

These small towns are so dull.

Just then, a young boy stepped out of the general store.

Who is that stranger in black? He looks scary.

Harvey called to the boy.

Hello there, friend!

Where might I find the rabbi of this fine town?

Sorry, what was that?

Harvey gave chase.

Can I talk to you for a second?

No.

At least tell me the rabbi's name. And make it quick!

Or else you'll beat me up?

No, or else I'll fall too far behind to hear.

Kid: There's no rabbi, no mayor, no sheriff.
Harvey: So who's in charge?

Kid: Big Milt.
Harvey: Where can I find him?
Kid: The saloon. Now stop chasing me!
Harvey: Okay.

No rabbi? This could be my lucky day.

Harvey found the saloon. He straightened his suit before entering.

He gave himself some advice: Remember not to appear over-anxious. Act like you could take or leave the job.

In the saloon:

... so King Solomon wanted a new ring. And he wanted it to have an inscription that would be fitting every time he read it, no matter what kind of mood he was in. Can you guess what his wise jeweler inscribed in the ring?

CRUNCH!

Matzah co.

This too shall pass.

The bar was silent.

I don't like the looks of this.

The stranger stepped forward.

I'm looking for a gentleman named "Big Milt."

Who is this clown? And how does he know about Solomon's ring?

You have found him, sir.

Greetings, sir. I am Rabbi Harvey from back East in New York. I have only recently graduated, but I was near the top of my class, and I am fully qualified to lead a small or even medium-sized congregation.

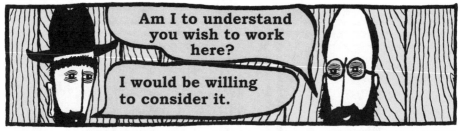

Am I to understand you wish to work here?

I would be willing to consider it.

Let me ask you, Rabbi ... I was sick the day of my bar mitzvah, and my parents decided to have it without me. Am I too old to have one now?

Here we go.

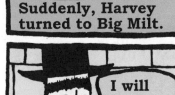

Hold on, though. If you shoot me, that means I lied when I said "I will hang today."

And?

And if I lied, I am to be hanged, not shot.

Are you following any of this?

You see the problem we have here? By your own rules, you can't hang me if I told the truth. And you can't shoot me if I lied.

The people were amazed. Big Milt was annoyed.

Who is this rabbi?

Very clever, kid.

Thanks, Milt.

I suppose you think I now have to let you go free?

That would be the honorable thing.

Aha! There's the flaw in your plan, smart guy! I *never* do the honorable thing! And I wasn't enjoying that game, anyway. Let's play a new one.

It's called "Dead Man's Delight." Do you want to know the rules?

Is it anything like baseball?

No. In this game, you choose how you want to die. And we make your wish come true. You have thirty seconds. Tick, tick....

Quiet, please.

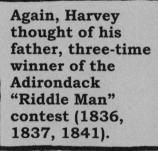

Again, Harvey thought of his father, three-time winner of the Adirondack "Riddle Man" contest (1836, 1837, 1841).

Is there a trick to this question, pop?

Let's hope so.

I think I've got it.

We'll see.

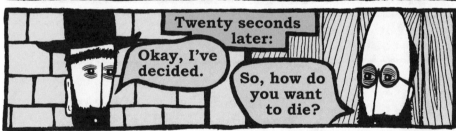

Twenty seconds later:

Okay, I've decided.

So, how do you want to die?

Of old age.

I'm just not getting anywhere with this guy.

The children were rooting for Harvey.

Now we have to stand here until he dies of old age.

Great. I was hoping to retire in the spring.

Big Milt began to lose his cool.

I'm trying to play fair with you, Rabbi, and you keep pulling these tricks.

Now tell me. Do you believe in God? And no witty answers, please.

Yes.

Good. Then we'll leave it in God's hands.

Big Milt addressed the people.

My friends, we will play one final game. I will take two pieces of paper. On one I will write "The Rabbi Lives." On the other I will write "The Rabbi Dies." I will put both pieces of paper in a hat, and our young visitor here will pick one without looking. And whatever that piece of paper says ... such will be his fate today.

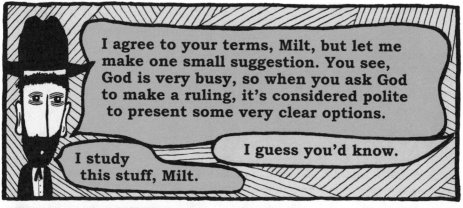

Big Milt called out for a piece of paper, but no one would give him one. So he grabbed a cardboard box from the street and ripped off two pieces and wrote something on each piece. Then he folded the pieces of cardboard and dropped them into a hat. He held out the hat. Harvey reached in ...

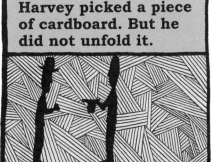

Harvey picked a piece of cardboard. But he did not unfold it.

Listen, Milt, I have a bad feeling about this. I mean, I didn't really sense much guidance from above while picking this paper. I might as well go ahead and make my final request right now. I'd like to eat one last piece of matzah.

Big Milt turned to the crowd.

Shall I grant this request?

Have a heart, Milt! Let the kid have a lousy piece of matzah!

Very well. For the sake of my people, I will grant your final wish.

Moses, a matzah if you please?

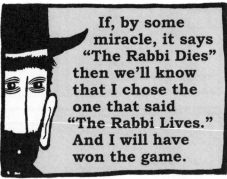

ONE HUNGRY RABBI

It was Friday afternoon, and the Rabbi was getting hungry.

Dream on, Rebbe.

But Rabbi Harvey had been traveling, and he was still many miles from home. He had nowhere to spend the Sabbath.

He got up and continued walking. "Hopefully," he said to himself, "some kind stranger will take me in for the night."

Just then, the Rabbi heard a wagon. The driver stopped.

How about a ride, sir?

Driver: Say, if you're not busy, why don't you join my wife and me for dinner?
Rabbi: Thank you. I would love to.
Driver: Magnificent. I just have to make one quick stop on the way home.

The man dropped the corn, turned, and sprinted back to the wagon. They sped off down the road.

When they were a mile away, the man slowed the wagon down.

I'm so ashamed.

Because you were stealing?

Yes. Also, now everyone can see me without my hat.

You should have seen me thirty years ago. I had such thick, curly hair. Just like King David, my wife used to say.

So who was it that saw me stealing? Old man Meyers?

No.

Who then, mister? I need to know who to avoid.

Yes, every spring I give a special Sabbath feast for all of my neighbors. I bought this cask of wine for tonight, but now it's nearly empty. Stolen, I suppose. There's nothing to do but cancel the feast.

Let's not be rash. Perhaps we can figure out what happened.

I bet my horse Fred drank it. I should go see if he's walking funny.

Ah-ha, I see.

Look at this, you've got a leak here in the bottom of the cask.

A leak in the bottom? That's impossible.

Why?

Well, there's still a tiny bit of wine at the bottom of the cask, isn't there?

Yes, so?

Don't you see? There's wine at the bottom of the cask, but none in the top. So if there's a leak, it has to be somewhere on the top.

The Rabbi was speechless.

He got up and brushed the dirt from his clothes.

You were correct, sir. This truly is a terrible tragedy. I wish you the best.

The Rabbi walked on. It was getting quite dark out. He was not exactly sure where he was anymore.

But soon he came to another house.

He knocked on the door. The door opened.

Good evening. My, what a lovely house you have.

Whatever you're selling, we don't want any.

No, you misunderstand. I am a rabbi.

Still, I really can't buy any-thing from you.

I am miles from home, and I have no place to spend the Sabbath.

I see, Rabbi. Yes, that is a real problem. Well, hmm, let's see.... You know what you should do?

What?

About three miles up this road is the home of a wealthy merchant. I'm sure he would be honored to have you as a guest.

Why did I marry this man?

The man said goodnight. Then he closed the door.

Harvey turned and began to walk away. Through the window he could hear the couple arguing.

How could you do it, Stan? How could you turn away a rabbi?

What do you want me to do, Doris? You know it's the Sabbath, and you know we can never remember all the prayers you're supposed to say. I would have been ashamed to have him here.

I guess you're right. Besides, we don't really have a meal fit for a rabbi. He's probably used to fancy Sabbath dinners. And we only have potatoes.

The Rabbi thought for a moment. He could walk three miles to the merchant's house ... but he had a better idea.

He returned to the door and knocked. Then he waited a very long time.

A cowboy's life is a weary, dreary life, Some say it's free from care ...

Rounding up cattle from morning till night, in the middle of the prairie so bare.

The Rabbi is back, Doris. Please get the door.

Me? You're the one who chased him away. You get it.

Come on, just tell him I was called away on business. In the meantime, I'll be hiding under the bed.

The Rabbi continued to wait.

And wait. Finally, the door opened.

Rabbi! What a nice surprise! We thought you left long ago!

Listen, I'm afraid I have to admit something.

Me too, Rabbi. Let me stop you both right there.

First allow *me* to admit something. I once ate at that rich merchant's house, the one three miles up the road. I'm not proud to say this, but ...

The food was lousy.

It was?

Sure. It was nothing but one fancy dish after another, all night long.

That sort of meal is not for me.

It's not?

No. You put a potato on a plate, I'm happy.

And another thing, since we're on the subject. We had quite an awkward disagreement over the Sabbath prayers, that merchant and I.

Did you really?

Uh-oh.

I'm afraid so.

You see, the merchant insisted upon saying all the prayers himself. He said he didn't enjoy the way I prayed. I don't like to stay with people who are not satisfied with my praying.

That's certainly understandable.

I mean, I'm a rabbi, after all. I don't tell him how to sell dry goods.

Forget about that merchant, Rabbi. Why don't you join us for dinner?

Yes, you must.

Thank you, I would like that.

We're having potatoes.

Potatoes! This is my lucky day!

FORGIVE ME, RABBI

If one man boxes another man's ear, or plucks his hair, what is the proper punishment? What if one man spits at another man so that the spittle reaches him? What then? These were some of the questions that sparked heated debate at the tenth annual Rocky Mountain Rabbi Convention in Cheyenne, Wyoming.

T'was out in old West Texas, boys, spring of '73, That a wealthy cattle driver came steppin' up to me, ♪ Sayin' "How do you do, young feller, and how'd you like to go, ♫ And spend a summer pleasantly on the trail to Mexico?"

When the convention ended, Rabbi Harvey stood by the road and waited for the stagecoach to Elk Spring.

Elk Spring in about three hours, gentlemen.

The stage finally came and Harvey got on. There were already two men seated in the coach.

In the stagecoach:

Hello there.

Howdy.

How do, old-timer?

Old-timer? Do I really look like an old-timer? It's probably just this long beard.

Why don't you join us in a few hands of cards, mister? We can play something nice and simple.

Not right now, thank you.

Oh, come on, pops. We'll even let you win once in a while.

Thanks, again. But I would really prefer to just sit quietly and do a little thinking.

I think this situation calls for the old "ignore him until he shuts up" trick.

Come on, mister, aren't you at least going to defend yourself? Where's your pride?

I'll do a little bird watching to pass the time. Look at that huge one up there. Is it an eagle? I really should know these things ...

So you're giving me the silent treatment, huh? Where do you get the nerve? You know, I've got half a mind to throw you right off this coach! That's what you deserve for ruining my good mood. What do you say to that, old man?

Ah, now there's a painted bunting. Or is it a wood duck? Wait, now that it's coming closer, I think it's a loon. This is very hard.

The man continued insulting and abusing Rabbi Harvey all the way to Elk Spring. But Harvey refused to respond. He just silently watched birds, identifying many of them incorrectly.

The wagon dropped Harvey off in town.

And stay out!

WICKERSHAM & CO. DRUG STORE

He was glad to be home.

Welcome back, Rabbi!

Good to be back, Josh.

ELK S[...]RY GOODS GEN[...]AL

We missed you, Rabbi!

Thanks, Laura.

In the wagon:

Why do they keep calling that old guy "Rabbi"?

I *thought* he looked familiar. He must have been that famous rabbi you always hear about.

You mean that was Rabbi Harvey of Elk Spring?

Yep.

Uh-oh.

The Rabbi walked through town.

Before I unpack, I have some important business to attend to.

Today we have roasted chicken, pan-fried steak, and fresh salmon.

One of each.

I'm not looking forward to this.

In the restaurant:

Rabbi Harvey?

Hello. I still don't want to play cards.

I feel terrible, Rabbi. Please forgive me for insulting you.

Sorry, I can't forgive you.

You can't?

No.

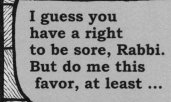

I guess you have a right to be sore, Rabbi. But do me this favor, at least ...

Can you tell me which prayers I need to say to get God to forgive me?

Why should God have to get involved? If you have wronged a fellow human being, you should go to that person for forgiveness.

That's great news!

Perhaps.

Tell me, who did you think that old-timer in the wagon was?

Just a regular guy. A blacksmith or something.

And you dared to talk to the blacksmith like that?

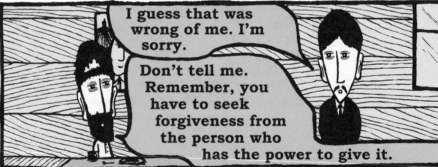

I guess that was wrong of me. I'm sorry.

Don't tell me. Remember, you have to seek forgiveness from the person who has the power to give it.

Meaning, the person you have wronged. You'll find his workshop behind the bakery.

I suggest you hurry.

YOU'RE A BRAVE MAN, HARVEY

Harvey grew up in a small town in the Adirondack Mountains of northern New York.

He never did very well in school. Maybe because he mostly looked out the window.

And never got his chores done on time either.

He always stopped in the middle and stared into space.

But when it came to daydreaming, there wasn't a kid in town who could beat him. He used to sit under his favorite tree for five hours at a time. He loved to imagine himself in all the great Bible stories.

Looks like rain again today, huh Noah?

Who is this kid?

Harvey started for town.

Two loaves of bread.
Two loaves of bread.
Two loaves of bread.
Two loaves of bread.
Two loaves of bread.
Two loaves of bread.
Two loaves of bread.

But Harvey was soon very bored. Next thing you know, young King David was walking along with him.

I'm on my way to fight Goliath to the death.

I'm on my way to the bakery.

They say he's nine feet tall and very grouchy.

I have a Hebrew teacher like that.

The boys stopped to watch a farmer working in his field.

That's Sy, the wheat farmer.

How interesting.

Sy called to Harvey.

What do you think of my field, Harvey?

Harvey said the first thing that came into his head.

Two loaves of bread!

What!

Are you mocking me, kid? Are you saying that all of my land will only produce two lousy loaves of bread? How dare you?

Sy picked up a stone.

Harvey ducked.

That's for saying my land is no good! What do you know about wheat farming, anyway?

Next time you pass a farm, you better say, "May you have an abundant harvest!"

May you have an abundant harvest!

I said next time, you fool!

Sy didn't follow through very well on his throw.

Luckily.

Once the neighbor's dog tried to eat my ant collection and I chased him away with a stick.

You're a brave man, Harvey.

Harvey came to the cemetery. A funeral was in progress. Harvey watched with great sadness.

There go the old Shaboshnik Brothers. I'll miss them. I feel like I should say something.

Away with the cursed things!

Did I say the wrong thing?

Probably.

I wonder why they're putting down the coffins?

Yes, that is quite sad. There's really only one thing I can say. May you be reunited in eternal heaven.

That's a horrible thing to say.

Thanks.

It is?

Do you want me to go to the cow section of heaven? Is that where you think I belong?

Next time, if you must speak, just say, "Ah, so this is how a cow is led to the slaughter-house."

Fine.

Anna led the cow onto Harvey's foot.

Ouch!

CRUNCH!!

Then she yelled back to him:

Double ouch.

And never ask me to a dance ever again!

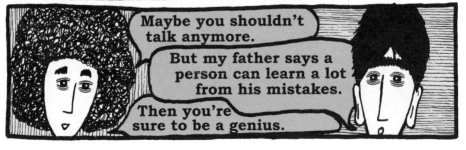

Maybe you shouldn't talk anymore.

But my father says a person can learn a lot from his mistakes.

Then you're sure to be a genius.

Excuse me for a minute.

Rabbi Sid took Harvey for a little walk.

Have you ever been to a wedding before, Harvey?

Yes, Rabbi.

Remember how after the ceremony they crushed a wine glass under their foot?

Sure, Rabbi.

I was just thinking ... perhaps this time we'll use your head.

To crush the glass?

No, instead of the glass.

Five minutes later.

Boy do I love Rabbi Sid! He explained everything to me.

Let's hope.

It's so simple ... I can't believe I never thought of it before.

Harvey was getting close to town.

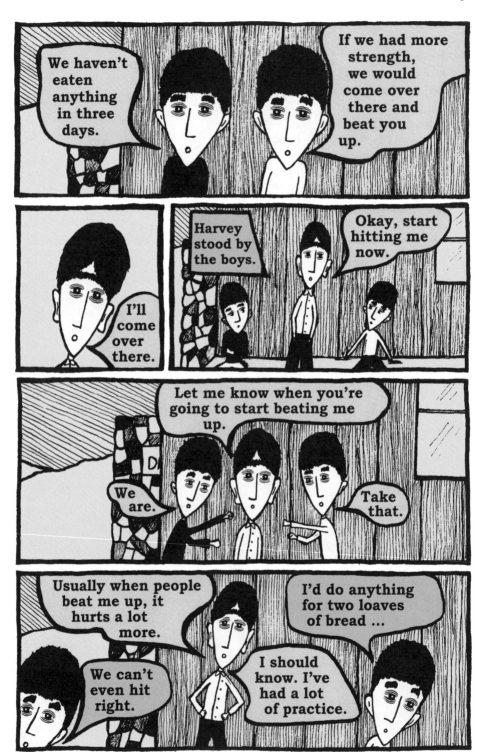

The boys didn't say anything. Actually, they seemed a little concerned. But they followed Harvey to the bakery.

Two loaves of bread for my friends, please!

Sure thing, Harvey. It's always a pleasure to serve a polite young man like yourself.

Harvey paid for the bread. The boys looked over the selection of freshly baked loaves for a long time.

Let's go, kids, I've got challahs in the oven.

Meanwhile, Harvey started home. Empty-handed.

I can't wait to tell my mom all about what happened!

I've said it before, and I'll say it again. You're a brave man, Harvey.

STUMP THE RABBI

I read and study quite a bit, Rabbi. But how will I know when I've finally become a wise man?

You'll know you are wise when you can learn something from a fool.

Who's next?

Year after year, the most popular event at the Elk Spring Fair was the "Stump the Rabbi" booth. For five cents, you could ask Rabbi Harvey any question. If he was unable to come up with the answer, you won a free pie—your choice of flavor. Very few pies were given out, however.

Rabbi, I barely earn a living.

STUMP THE RABBI 5¢

ELIXIR CO.

Yet I work very hard all day. Is this fair?

The Bible teaches that only by the sweat of your brow shall you eat bread.

I have a follow-up. Here's another nickel.

I'm listening.

For all the sweat that comes out of my brow, don't you think I deserve a lot more bread?

It's not healthy to eat heavily after exercise.

Here's a tough one, Rabbi H. How many trees are there in Colorado?

28,764,625

Are you sure?

Go count them and see.

Next!

I wish to marry a certain man, Rabbi, but he is very short. I mean, he's about this high. What should I do?

Bend down to hear him.

Rabbi, I am Nathan, former candle maker, former teacher, current sugar beet farmer.

I remember you well.

Here is my worry. How can I ever live up to the example set by great men like Moses?

I sometimes have the same concern, but I look at it this way. In the world to come, I will not be asked, "Why weren't you Moses?" But I might be asked, "Why weren't you Harvey?"

The thing is, Rabbi, I think I understand how a person should live. How to honor and respect others and do the right thing and all that. But it takes so much effort. Do I really have to start so young?

Certainly not. Wait until the day before you die.

But I don't know when that will be. I'm only ten years old.

I see. In that case, start today.

Okay, Rabbi, say I wanted to carry a card with me in my pocket. Something that would always remind me of what is important. What would I write on the card?

On one side of the card, write: The universe was created for me.

On the other side, write: I was created from dust.

I'll admit it, Rabbi, we came out West to try to get rich. We had a fruit farm in Oregon, then a dry goods store in Seattle, then a hotel in Denver. We've done alright, but ... where is the fortune we came out here to find?

You've been chasing after your fortune, but what if it's not in front of you? It could be behind you, in which case you need to slow down and let it catch up.

That, or try silver mining.

The last question of the afternoon was the most difficult.

Something has been bothering me, Rabbi.

Yes, Albert?

Slavery, the Civil War, stealing land from Indians.... How could all these things happen in our country? I don't understand.... Where was God?

Rabbi Harvey thought for a moment. Then he responded with a question of his own.

This got them both to thinking.

Where were people?

BAD *BUBBE*

In a small town in northern Colorado, there lived two brothers named George and Harry. They were both merchants, but they could never agree on what to sell. So they divided their store, as you see below.

One day, Harry, who ran the wine-selling half of the store, realized that he was all out of wine. The truth is, Harry was not really the most clever merchant in the West.

Doesn't it seem like I just bought a couple hundred cases? Oh, no, that was last year. No wonder I'm all out.

Harry planned a wine-buying trip.

I know my customers enjoyed that Elk Spring wine ...

Harry called across the store.

Hey Georgie, I'm going on a trip! You need anything? Maybe a nice book or something?

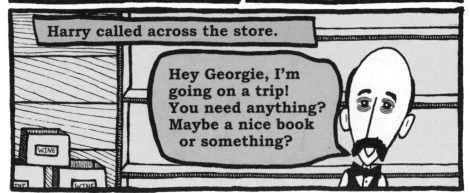

George insisted upon seeing Harry's note about Abe Lincoln and the Haggadahs. The bookseller had once requested books about the American Revolution. His brother brought back six volumes on the art of making goat cheese.

The next day, Harry set out on his trip. He made a wrong turn at Gooseneck Ridge, but soon got back on the road toward Elk Spring.

In the city of Denver, there lately did dwell, a topping wine merchant, that's known very well....

Two days later, he arrived in Elk Spring. He liked the looks of *Bubbe's* Inn, so he decided to stay there.

That's new.

Good afternoon. I'm Harry the wine merchant. You must be *Bubbe.*

How did you guess?

I have a very cozy room upstairs. Meet my grand-daughter.

Welcome, I'm Rachel.

Bubbe showed Harry the cozy room.

Say, that's cozy.

Harry took out his stack of money and paid for two nights. *Bubbe* and Rachel went downstairs. Harry looked around his room. It did not take long.

The Rabbi walked home after dinner. Harry went up to his room and changed into his pajamas. At about midnight, he heard noises coming from below the window—whispers and the sounds of digging. But he ignored the noises and continued reading from Proverbs.

Do not gulp down the wine, the strong red wine ...

Uh-oh.

Soon the noises stopped.

Harry waited another hour, and then went outside.

This is the right spot, isn't it?

He started digging. The money was there.

I missed you.

He tiptoed upstairs, packed his bag, and left *Bubbe's* Inn. He rode into town and knocked on the wine maker's door.

Open up! It's the wine merchant!

This better be good.

I have your money.

Come back in the morning.

Well, the thing is, I didn't really like the inn where I was staying. So I thought it might be fun to stay here.

The wine maker did not agree that it would be fun, but he was too tired to argue. There was only one bed, so they had to share.

Say, do you have another one of those fancy night caps?

Never speak again.

Harry closed his eyes.

Maybe in the morning you can show me how to make wine.

Get out.

Back at the inn, *Bubbe* was doing a little digging in the pale moonlight.

Let's see ... six hundred dollars, plus a much larger sum, equals ... well, a lot!

She dug and dug, but found nothing.

She soon realized that there was nothing to find.

I've been tricked by the Rabbi! He'll never eat at my inn again!

The Rabbi watched from a spot on a nearby hill. He was glad to see justice done.

But he was sorry to hear that he was no longer welcome at the inn. He had actually enjoyed the pot roast greatly.

It's not always easy to be the Rabbi.

SUGGESTIONS FOR FURTHER READING

Certner, Simon, ed. *101 Jewish Stories: A Treasury of Folktales from Midrash and Other Sources*. New York: Board of Jewish Education of Greater New York, 1983.

Eisner, Will. *The Plot: The Secret Story of the Protocols of the Elders of Zion*. New York: W. W. Norton, 2006.

Kaplan, Aryeh, trans. *The Lost Princess & Other Kabbalistic Tales of Rebbe Nachman of Breslov*. Woodstock, VT: Jewish Lights, 2005.

———. *The Seven Beggars & Other Kabbalistic Tales of Rebbe Nachman of Breslov*. Woodstock, VT: Jewish Lights, 2005.

Katchor, Ben. *The Jew of New York*. New York: Pantheon, 2000.

Mack, Stan. *The Story of the Jews: A 4,000-Year Adventure—A Graphic History Book*. Woodstock, VT: Jewish Lights, 2001.

Rochlin, Fred and Harriet. *Pioneer Jews: A New Life in the Far West*. Boston: Houghton Mifflin, 1986.

Sheinkin, David. *Path of the Kabbalah*. New York: Paragon House, 1986.

Sheinkin, Steve. *Rabbi Harvey Rides Again: A Graphic Novel of Jewish Folktales Let Loose in the Wild West*. Woodstock, VT: Jewish Lights, 2008.

———. *Rabbi Harvey vs. the Wisdom Kid: A Graphic Novel of Dueling Jewish Folktales in the Wild West*. Woodstock, VT: Jewish Lights, 2010.

Spiegelman, Art. *Maus: A Survivor's Tale: My Father Bleeds History/Here My Troubles Began*. New York: Pantheon, 1991.

Waldman, JT. *Megillat Esther*. Philadelphia: Jewish Publication Society, 2006.

Wiesel, Elie. *Souls on Fire: Portraits and Legends of Hasidic Masters*. New York: Simon & Schuster, 1982.

Bible Study / Midrash

Passing Life's Tests: Spiritual Reflections on the Trial of Abraham, the Binding of Isaac *By Rabbi Bradley Shavit Artson, DHL*
Invites us to use this powerful tale as a tool for our own soul wrestling, to confront our existential sacrifices and enable us to face—and surmount—life's tests.
6 x 9, 176 pp, Quality PB, 978-1-58023-631-7 **$18.99**

Speaking Torah: Spiritual Teachings from around the Maggid's Table—in Two Volumes *By Arthur Green, with Ebn Leader, Ariel Evan Mayse and Or N. Rose*
The most powerful Hasidic teachings made accessible—from some of the world's preeminent authorities on Jewish thought and spirituality.
Volume 1—6 x 9, 512 pp, HC, 978-1-58023-668-3 **$34.99**
Volume 2—6 x 9, 448 pp, HC, 978-1-58023-694-2 **$34.99**

A Partner in Holiness: Deepening Mindfulness, Practicing Compassion and Enriching Our Lives through the Wisdom of R. Levi Yitzhak of Berdichev's *Kedushat Levi*
By Rabbi Jonathan P. Slater, DMin; Foreword by Arthur Green; Preface by Rabby Nancy Flam
Contemporary mindfulness and classical Hasidic spirituality are brought together to inspire a satisfying spiritual life of practice.
Volume 1— 6 x 9, 336 pp, HC, 978-1-58023-794-9 **$35.00**
Volume 2— 6 x 9, 288 pp, HC, 978-1-58023-795-6 **$35.00**

The Genesis of Leadership: What the Bible Teaches Us about Vision, Values an Leading Change *By Rabbi Nathan Laufer; Foreword by Senator Joseph I. Lieberman*
6 x 9, 288 pp, Quality PB, 978-1-58023-352-1 **$18.99**

Hineini in Our Lives: Learning How to Respond to Others through 14 Biblical Texts and Personal Stories *By Dr. Norman J. Cohen* 6 x 9, 240 pp, Quality PB, 978-1-58023-274-6 **$18.99**

Masking and Unmasking Ourselves: Interpreting Biblical Texts on Clothing & Identity *By Dr. Norman J. Cohen* 6 x 9, 224 pp, HC, 978-1-58023-461-0 **$24.99**
Quality PB, 978-1-58023-839-7 **$18.99**

The Messiah and the Jews: Three Thousand Years of Tradition, Belief and Hope
By Rabbi Elaine Rose Glickman; Foreword by Rabbi Neil Gillman, PhD
Preface by Rabbi Judith Z. Abrams, PhD 6 x 9, 192 pp, Quality PB, 978-1-58023-690-4 **$16.99**

The Modern Men's Torah Commentary: New Insights from Jewish Men on th 54 Weekly Torah Portions *Edited by Rabbi Jeffrey K. Salkin*
6 x 9, 368 pp, HC, 978-1-58023-395-8 **$24.99**

Moses and the Journey to Leadership: Timeless Lessons of Effective Management from the Bible and Today's Leaders *By Dr. Norman J. Cohen*
6 x 9, 240 pp, Quality PB, 978-1-58023-351-4 **$18.99**; HC, 978-1-58023-227-2 **$21.99**

The Other Talmud—The *Yerushalmi*: Unlocking the Secrets of *The Talmud of Israel* for Judaism Today *By Rabbi Judith Z. Abrams, PhD*
6 x 9, 256 pp, HC, 978-1-58023-463-4 **$24.99**

Sage Tales: Wisdom and Wonder from the Rabbis of the Talmud
By Rabbi Burton L. Visotzky
6 x 9, 256 pp, Quality PB, 978-1-58023-791-8 **$19.99**; HC, 978-1-58023-456-6 **$24.99**

The Torah Revolution: Fourteen Truths That Changed the World
By Rabbi Reuven Hammer, PhD 6 x 9, 240 pp, Quality PB, 978-1-58023-789-5 **$18.99**
HC, 978-1-58023-457-3 **$24.99**

The Wisdom of Judaism: An Introduction to the Values of the Talmud
By Rabbi Dov Peretz Elkins 6 x 9, 192 pp, Quality PB, 978-1-58023-327-9 **$16.99**

JEWISH LIGHTS is an imprint of

TURNER
PUBLISHING COMPANY

Spirituality / Crafts

Beading—The Creative Spirit: Finding Your Sacred Center through the Art of Beadwork *By Wendy Ellsworth*
7 x 9, 240 pp, 8-page full-color insert, b/w photos and diagrams, Quality PB, 978-1-59473-267-6 **$18.99***

Contemplative Crochet: A Hands-On Guide for Interlocking Faith and Craft
By Cindy Crandall-Frazier; Foreword by Linda Skolnik
7 x 9, 208 pp, b/w photos and diagrams, Quality PB, 978-1-59473-238-6 **$16.99***

Jewish Threads: A Hands-On Guide to Stitching Spiritual Intention into Jewish Fabric Crafts *By Diana Drew with Robert Grayson*
7 x 9, 288 pp, 8-page full-color insert, b/w illus. and photos, Quality PB, 978-1-58023-442-9 **$19.99**

The Knitting Way: A Guide to Spiritual Self-Discovery
By Linda Skolnik and Janice MacDaniels
7 x 9, 240 pp, b/w photos and diagrams, Quality PB, 978-1-59473-079-5 **$16.99***

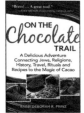

The Painting Path: Embodying Spiritual Discovery through Yoga, Brush and Color
By Linda Novick; Foreword by Richard Segalman
7 x 9, 208 pp, 8-page full-color insert, b/w photos and illus., Quality PB, 978-1-59473-226-3 **$18.99***

The Quilting Path: A Guide to Spiritual Self-Discovery through Fabric, Thread and Kabbalah
By Louise Silk 7 x 9, 192 pp, b/w photos and diagrams, Quality PB, 978-1-59473-206-5 **$16.99***

Travel / History

Israel—A Spiritual Travel Guide, 2nd Edition: A Companion for the Modern Jewish Pilgrim *By Rabbi Lawrence A. Hoffman, PhD*
Helps today's pilgrim tap into the deep spiritual meaning of the ancient—and modern—sites of the Holy Land.
4¾ x 10, 256 pp, Illus., Quality PB, 978-1-58023-261-6 **$19.99**
Also Available: **The Israel Mission Leader's Guide** 5½ x 8½, 16 pp, PB, 978-1-58023-085-8 **$4.95**

On the Chocolate Trail: A Delicious Adventure Connecting Jews, Religions, History, Travel, Rituals and Recipes to the Magic of Cacao
By Rabbi Deborah R. Prinz
Take a delectable journey through the religious history of chocolate—a real treat!
6 x 9, 272 pp, 20+ b/w photographs, Quality PB, 978-1-58023-487-0 **$18.99**

Twelve Steps

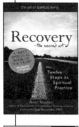

Recovery, the 12 Steps and Jewish Spirituality
Reclaiming Hope, Courage & Wholeness
By Rabbi Paul Steinberg; Foreword by Rabbi Abraham J. Twerski, MD; Preface by Harriet Rossetto
The first comprehensive approach to successfully integrate traditional Jewish wisdom and spirituality with the experience, strength and hope of the 12 Steps of Alcoholics Anonymous (AA). 6 x 9, 176 pp, Quality PB, 978-1-58023-808-3 **$16.99**

Recovery—The Sacred Art: The Twelve Steps as Spiritual Practice
By Rami Shapiro; Foreword by Joan Borysenko, PhD
Draws on insights and practices of different religious traditions to help you move more deeply into the universal spirituality of the Twelve Step system.
5½ x 8½, 240 pp, Quality PB, 978-1-59473-259-1 **$16.99***

100 Blessings Every Day: Daily Twelve Step Recovery Affirmations, Exercises for Personal Growth & Renewal Reflecting Seasons of the Jewish Year
By Rabbi Kerry M. Olitzky; Foreword by Rabbi Neil Gillman, PhD
4½ x 6½, 432 pp, Quality PB, 978-1-879045-30-9 **$18.99**

Recovery from Codependence: A Jewish Twelve Steps Guide to Healing Your Soul
By Rabbi Kerry M. Olitzky 6 x 9, 160 pp, Quality PB, 978-1-879045-32-3 **$13.95**

Twelve Jewish Steps to Recovery, 2nd Edition: A Personal Guide to Turning from Alcoholism & Other Addictions—Drugs, Food, Gambling, Sex ...
By Rabbi Kerry M. Olitzky and Stuart A. Copans, MD; Preface by Abraham J. Twerski, MD
6 x 9, 160 pp, Quality PB, 978-1-58023-409-2 **$18.99**

*A book from SkyLight Paths, Jewish Lights' sister imprint

Theology / Philosophy / The Way Into... Series

The Way Into... series offers an accessible and highly usable "guided tour" of the Jewish faith, people, history and beliefs—in total, an introduction to Judaism that will enable you to understand and interact with the sacred texts of the Jewish tradition. Each volume is written by a leading contemporary scholar and teacher, and explores one key aspect of Judaism. The Way Into... series enables all readers to achieve a real sense of Jewish cultural literacy through guided study.

The Way Into Encountering God in Judaism
By Rabbi Neil Gillman, PhD
For everyone who wants to understand how Jews have encountered God throughout history and today.
6 x 9, 240 pp, Quality PB, 978-1-58023-199-2 **$18.99**; HC, 978-1-58023-025-4 **$21.95**
Also Available: **The Jewish Approach to God:** A Brief Introduction for Christians
By Rabbi Neil Gillman, PhD
5½ x 8½, 192 pp, Quality PB, 978-1-58023-190-9 **$18.99**

The Way Into Jewish Mystical Tradition
By Rabbi Lawrence Kushner
Allows readers to interact directly with the sacred mystical texts of the Jewish tradition. An accessible introduction to the concepts of Jewish mysticism, their religious and spiritual significance, and how they relate to life today.
6 x 9, 224 pp, Quality PB, 978-1-58023-200-5 **$18.99**

The Way Into Jewish Prayer
By Rabbi Lawrence A. Hoffman, PhD
Opens the door to 3,000 years of Jewish prayer, making anyone feel at home in the Jewish way of communicating with God.
6 x 9, 208 pp, Quality PB, 978-1-58023-201-2 **$18.99**

The Way Into Jewish Prayer Teacher's Guide
By Rabbi Jennifer Ossakow Goldsmith
8½ x 11, 42 pp, PB, 978-1-58023-345-3 **$8.99**
Download a free copy at www.jewishlights.com.

The Way Into Judaism and the Environment
By Jeremy Benstein, PhD
Explores the ways in which Judaism contributes to contemporary social-environmental issues, the extent to which Judaism is part of the problem and how it can be part of the solution.
6 x 9, 288 pp, Quality PB, 978-1-58023-368-2 **$18.99**; HC, 978-1-58023-268-5 **$24.99**

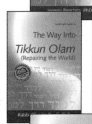

The Way Into *Tikkun Olam* (Repairing the World)
By Rabbi Elliot N. Dorff, PhD
An accessible introduction to the Jewish concept of the individual's responsibility to care for others and repair the world.
6 x 9, 304 pp, Quality PB, 978-1-58023-328-6 **$18.99**

The Way Into Torah
By Rabbi Norman J. Cohen, PhD
Helps guide you in the exploration of the origins and development of Torah, explains why it should be studied and how to do it.
6 x 9, 176 pp, Quality PB, 978-1-58023-198-5 **$16.99**

The Way Into the Varieties of Jewishness
By Sylvia Barack Fishman, PhD
Explores the religious and historical understanding of what it has meant to be Jewish from ancient times to the present controversy over "Who is a Jew?"
6 x 9, 288 pp, Quality PB, 978-1-58023-367-5 **$18.99**; HC, 978-1-58023-030-8 **$24.99**

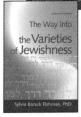

Children's Books

Lullaby
By Debbie Friedman; Full-color illus. by Lorraine Bubar

A charming adaptation of beloved singer-songwriter Debbie Friedman's best-selling song *Lullaby*, this timeless bedtime picture book will help children know that God will keep them safe throughout the night.

9 x 12, 32 pp, Full-color illus., w/ a CD of original music & lyrics by Debbie Friedman
HC, 978-1-58023-807-6 **$18.99** *For ages 3–6*

Around the World in One Shabbat
Jewish People Celebrate the Sabbath Together
By Durga Yael Bernhard

Takes your child on a colorful adventure to share the many ways Jewish people celebrate Shabbat around the world.

11 x 8½, 32 pp, Full-color illus., HC, 978-1-58023-433-7 **$18.99** *For ages 3–6*

It's a ... It's a ... It's a Mitzvah
By Liz Suneby and Diane Heiman; Full-color illus. by Laurel Molk

Join Mitzvah Meerkat and friends as they introduce children to the everyday kindnesses that mark the beginning of a Jewish journey and a lifetime commitment to *tikkun olam* (repairing the world).

9 x 12, 32 pp, Full-color illus., HC, 978-1-58023-509-9 **$18.99** *For ages 3–6*

Also Available as a Board Book: **That's a Mitzvah**
5 x 5, 24 pp, Full-color illus., Board Book, 978-1-58023-804-5 **$8.99** *For ages 1–4*

What You Will See Inside a Synagogue
By Rabbi Lawrence A. Hoffman, PhD, and Dr. Ron Wolfson; Full-color photos by Bill Aron

A colorful, fun-to-read introduction that explains the ways and whys of Jewish worship and religious life.

8½ x 10½, 32 pp, Full-color photos, Quality PB, 978-1-59473-256-0 **$8.99*** *For ages 6 & up*

Because Nothing Looks Like God
By Lawrence Kushner and Karen Kushner

Invites parents and children to explore, together, the questions we all have about God.

11 x 8¾, 32 pp, Full-color illus., HC, 978-1-58023-092-6 **$18.99** *For ages 4 & up*

In God's Hands *By Lawrence Kushner and Gary Schmidt*

Each of us has the power to make the world a better place—working ordinary miracles with our everyday deeds.

9 x 12, 32 pp, Full-color illus., HC, 978-1-58023-224-1 **$16.99** *For ages 5 & up*

What Makes Someone a Jew? *By Lauren Seidman*

Reflects the changing face of American Judaism. Helps preschoolers and young readers understand that you don't have to look a certain way to be Jewish.

10 x 8½, 32 pp, Full-color photos, Quality PB, 978-1-58023-321-7 **$8.99** *For ages 3–6*

In Our Image: God's First Creatures
By Nancy Sohn Swartz God asks all of nature to offer gifts to humankind—with a promise that the humans would care for creation in return.

Full-color illus., eBook, 978-1-58023-520-4 **$16.95** *For ages 5 & up*
Animated app available on Apple App Store and the Google Play Marketplace **$9.99**

The Book of Miracles: A Young Person's Guide to Jewish Spiritual Awareness
Written and illus. by Lawrence Kushner
6 x 9, 96 pp, 2-color illus., HC, 978-1-879045-78-1 **$16.95** *For ages 9–13*

The Jewish Family Fun Book, 2nd Edition: Holiday Projects,
Everyday Activities, and Travel Ideas with Jewish Themes *By Danielle Dardashti and Roni Sarig*
6 x 9, 304 pp, w/ 70+ b/w illus., Quality PB, 978-1-58023-333-0 **$18.99**

When a Grandparent Dies: A Kid's Own Remembering Workbook for
Dealing with Shiva and the Year Beyond *By Nechama Liss-Levinson*
8 x 10, 48 pp, 2-color text, HC, 978-1-879045-44-6 **$15.95** *For ages 7–13*

*A book from SkyLight Paths, Jewish Lights' sister imprint

Children's Books by Sandy Eisenberg Sasso

The *Shema* in the Mezuzah
Listening to Each Other
Introduces children ages 3 to 6 to the words of the *Shema* and the custom of putting up the mezuzah. Winner, National Jewish Book Award.
9 x 12, 32 pp, Full-color illus., HC, 978-1-58023-506-8 **$18.99** *For ages 3–6*

Adam & Eve's First Sunset
God's New Day
Explores fear and hope, faith and gratitude in ways that will delight kids and adults—inspiring us to bless each of God's days and nights.
9 x 12, 32 pp, Full-color illus., HC, 978-1-58023-177-0 **$17.95** *For ages 4 & up*
Also Available as a Board Book: **Adam and Eve's New Day**
5 x 5, 24 pp, Full-color illus., Board Book, 978-1-59473-205-8 **$7.99*** *For ages 1–4*

But God Remembered
Stories of Women from Creation to the Promised Land
Four different stories of women—Lilith, Serach, Bityah and the Daughters of Z—teach us important values through their faith and actions.
9 x 12, 32 pp, Full-color illus., Quality PB, 978-1-58023-372-9 **$8.99** *For ages 8 & up*

For Heaven's Sake
Heaven is often found where you least expect it.
9 x 12, 32 pp, Full-color illus., HC, 978-1-58023-054-4 **$16.95** *For ages 4 & up*

God Said Amen
An inspiring story about hearing the answers to our prayers.
9 x 12, 32 pp, Full-color illus., HC, 978-1-58023-080-3 **$16.95** *For ages 4 & up*

God's Paintbrush: Special 10th Anniversary Edition
Wonderfully interactive, invites children of all faiths and backgrounds to encounter God through moments in their own lives. Provides questions adult and child can explore together. 11 x 8¼, 32 pp, Full-color illus., HC, 978-1-58023-195-4 **$18.99** *For ages 4 & up*
Also Available as a Board Book: **I Am God's Paintbrush**
5 x 5, 24 pp, Full-color illus., Board Book, 978-1-59473-265-2 **$7.99*** *For ages 1–4*
Also Available: **God's Paintbrush Teacher's Guide**
8½ x 11, 32 pp, PB, 978-1-879045-57-6 **$8.95**

God's Paintbrush Celebration Kit:
A Spiritual Activity Kit for Teachers and Students of All Faiths, All Backgrounds
9½ x 12, 40 Full-color Activity Sheets & Teacher Folder w/ complete instructions
HC, 978-1-58023-050-6 **$21.95**
8-Student Activity Sheet Pack (40 sheets/5 sessions), 978-1-58023-058-2 **$19.95**
Single-Student Activity Sheet Pack (5 sessions), 978-1-58023-059-9 **$3.95**

In God's Name
Like an ancient myth in its poetic text and vibrant illustrations, this award-winning modern fable about the search for God's name celebrates the diversity and, at the same time, the unity of all people.
9 x 12, 32 pp, Full-color illus., HC, 978-1-879045-26-2 **$18.99** *For ages 4 & up*
Also Available as a Board Book: **What Is God's Name?**
5 x 5, 24 pp, Full-color illus., Board Book, 978-1-893361-10-2 **$8.99*** *For ages 1–4*
Also Available in Spanish: **El nombre de Dios**
9 x 12, 32 pp, Full-color illus., HC, 978-1-893361-63-8 **$16.95** *For ages 4 & up*

Noah's Wife
The Story of Naamah
When God tells Noah to bring the animals of the world onto the ark, God also calls on Naamah, Noah's wife, to save each plant on earth.
9 x 12, 32 pp, Full-color illus., HC, 978-1-58023-134-3 **$16.95** *For ages 4 & up*
Also Available as a Board Book: **Naamah, Noah's Wife**
5 x 5, 24 pp, Full-color illus., Board Book, 978-1-893361-56-0 **$7.95*** *For ages 1–4*

**A book from SkyLight Paths, Jewish Lights' sister imprint*

Spirituality

The Rhythms of Jewish Living
A Sephardic Exploration of Judaism's Spirituality
By Rabbi Marc D. Angel, PhD Reclaims the natural, balanced and insightful teachings of Sephardic Judaism that can and should imbue modern Jewish spirituality.
6 x 9, 208 pp, Quality PB, 978-1-58023-834-2 **$18.99**

God and the Big Bang, 2nd Edition
Discovering Harmony between Science and Spirituality
By Daniel C. Matt Updated and expanded. Draws on the insights of physics and Kabbalah to uncover the sense of wonder and oneness that connects humankind with the universe and God. 6 x 9, 224 pp (est), Quality PB, 978-1-58023-836-6 **$18.99**

Amazing Chesed: Living a Grace-Filled Judaism
By Rabbi Rami Shapiro Drawing from ancient and contemporary, traditional and non-traditional Jewish wisdom, reclaims the idea of grace in Judaism.
6 x 9, 176 pp, Quality PB, 978-1-58023-624-9 **$16.99**

Perennial Wisdom for the Spiritually Independent: Sacred Teachings—
Annotated & Explained *Annotation by Rabbi Rami Shapiro; Foreword by Richard Rohr*
Weaves sacred texts and teachings from the world's major religions into a coherent exploration of the five core questions at the heart of every religion's search.
5½ x 8½, 336 pp, Quality PB, 978-1-59473-515-8 **$16.99***

A Book of Life: Embracing Judaism as a Spiritual Practice
By Rabbi Michael Strassfeld 6 x 9, 544 pp, Quality PB, 978-1-58023-247-0 **$24.99**

Bringing the Psalms to Life: How to Understand and Use the Book of Psalms
By Rabbi Daniel F. Polish, PhD 6 x 9, 208 pp, Quality PB, 978-1-58023-157-2 **$18.99**

Does the Soul Survive? 2nd Edition: A Jewish Journey to Belief in Afterlife, Past Lives
& Living with Purpose *By Rabbi Elie Kaplan Spitz; Foreword by Brian L. Weiss, MD*
6 x 9, 288 pp, Quality PB, 978-1-58023-818-2 **$18.99**

First Steps to a New Jewish Spirit: Reb Zalman's Guide to Recapturing the Intimacy &
Ecstasy in Your Relationship with God *By Rabbi Zalman Schachter-Shalomi (z"l) with Donald Gropman*
6 x 9, 144 pp, Quality PB, 978-1-58023-182-4 **$16.95**

Foundations of Sephardic Spirituality: The Inner Life of Jews of the Ottoman Empire
By Rabbi Marc D. Angel, PhD 6 x 9, 224 pp, Quality PB, 978-1-58023-341-5 **$18.99**

The God Upgrade: Finding Your 21st-Century Spirituality in Judaism's 5,000-Year-
Old Tradition *By Rabbi Jamie Korngold; Foreword by Rabbi Harold M. Schulweis*
6 x 9, 176 pp, Quality PB, 978-1-58023-443-6 **$15.99**

The Jewish Lights Spirituality Handbook: A Guide to Understanding, Exploring &
Living a Spiritual Life *Edited by Stuart M. Matlins*
6 x 9, 456 pp, Quality PB, 978-1-58023-093-3 **$19.99**

Jewish with Feeling: A Guide to Meaningful Jewish Practice
By Rabbi Zalman Schachter-Shalomi (z"l) with Joel Segel
5½ x 8½, 288 pp, Quality PB, 978-1-58023-691-1 **$19.99**

Judaism, Physics and God: Searching for Sacred Metaphors in a Post-Einstein World
By Rabbi David W. Nelson
6 x 9, 352 pp, Quality PB, inc. reader's discussion guide, 978-1-58023-306-4 **$18.99**
HC, 352 pp, 978-1-58023-252-4 **$24.99**

Repentance: The Meaning and Practice of Teshuvah
By Dr. Louis E. Newman; Foreword by Rabbi Harold M. Schulweis; Preface by Rabbi Karyn D. Kedar
6 x 9, 256 pp, HC, 978-1-58023-426-9 **$24.99**; Quality PB, 978-1-58023-718-5 **$18.99**

Tanya, the Masterpiece of Hasidic Wisdom: Selections Annotated & Explained
Translation & Annotation by Rabbi Rami Shapiro; Foreword by Rabbi Zalman Schachter-Shalomi (z"l)
5½ x 8½, 240 pp, Quality PB, 978-1-59473-275-1 **$18.99**

These Are the Words, 2nd Edition: A Vocabulary of Jewish Spiritual Life
By Rabbi Arthur Green, PhD 6 x 9, 320 pp, Quality PB, 978-1-58023-494-8 **$19.99**

Your Word Is Fire: The Hasidic Masters on Contemplative Prayer
Edited and translated by Rabbi Arthur Green, PhD, and Barry W. Holtz
6 x 9, 160 pp, Quality PB, 978-1-879045-25-5 **$16.99**

**A book from SkyLight Paths, Jewish Lights' sister imprint*

Inspiration

The Best Boy in the United States of America
A Memoir of Blessings and Kisses *By Dr. Ron Wolfson*
Filled with stories of growing up in a warm family, embracing Jewish identity and learning never to underestimate his mother, this moving memoir will resonate with anyone seeking to shape stronger families and communities and live a life of joy and purpose. 6 x 9, 192 pp, HC, 978-1-58023-838-0 **$19.99**

The Chutzpah Imperative: Empowering Today's Jews for a Life
That Matters *By Rabbi Edward Feinstein; Foreword by Rabbi Laura Geller*
A new view of chutzpah as Jewish self-empowerment to be God's partner and repair the world. Reveals Judaism's ancient message, its deepest purpose and most precious treasures. 6 x 9, 192 pp, HC, 978-1-58023-792-5 **$21.99**

Judaism's Ten Best Ideas: A Brief Guide for Seekers
By Rabbi Arthur Green, PhD A highly accessible introduction to Judaism's greatest contributions to civilization, drawing on Jewish mystical tradition and the author's experience. 4½ x 6½, 112 pp, Quality PB, 978-1-58023-803-8 **$9.99**

The Empty Chair: Finding Hope and Joy—Timeless Wisdom from a Hasidic Master,
Rebbe Nachman of Breslov *Adapted by Moshe Mykoff and the Breslov Research Institute*
4 x 6, 128 pp, Deluxe PB w/ flaps, 978-1-879045-67-5 **$9.99**

The Gentle Weapon: Prayers for Everyday and Not-So-Everyday Moments—
Timeless Wisdom from the Teachings of the Hasidic Master Rebbe Nachman of Breslov
Adapted by Moshe Mykoff and S. C. Mizrahi, together with the Breslov Research Institute
4 x 6, 144 pp, Deluxe PB w/ flaps, 978-1-58023-022-3 **$9.99**

God Whispers: Stories of the Soul, Lessons of the Heart *By Rabbi Karyn D. Kedar*
6 x 9, 176 pp, Quality PB, 978-1-58023-088-9 **$16.99**

God's To-Do List: 103 Ways to Be an Angel and Do God's Work on Earth
By Dr. Ron Wolfson 6 x 9, 144 pp, Quality PB, 978-1-58023-301-9 **$16.99**

Happiness and the Human Spirit: The Spirituality of Becoming the Best You Can Be
By Rabbi Abraham J. Twerski, MD
6 x 9, 176 pp, Quality PB, 978-1-58023-404-7 **$16.99**; HC, 978-1-58023-343-9 **$19.99**

Life's Daily Blessings: Inspiring Reflections on Gratitude and Joy for Every Day, Based
on Jewish Wisdom *By Rabbi Kerry M. Olitzky* 4½ x 6½, 368 pp, Quality PB, 978-1-58023-396-5 **$16.99**

Restful Reflections: Nighttime Inspiration to Calm the Soul, Based on Jewish Wisdom
By Rabbi Kerry M. Olitzky and Rabbi Lori Forman-Jacobi
4½ x 6½, 448 pp, Quality PB, 978-1-58023-091-9 **$16.99**

Sacred Intentions: Morning Inspiration to Strengthen the Spirit, Based on Jewish Wisdom
By Rabbi Kerry M. Olitzky and Rabbi Lori Forman-Jacobi
4½ x 6½, 448 pp, Quality PB, 978-1-58023-061-2 **$16.99**

Saying No and Letting Go: Jewish Wisdom on Making Room for What Matters Most
By Rabbi Edwin Goldberg, DHL; Foreword by Rabbi Naomi Levy
6 x 9, 192 pp, Quality PB, 978-1-58023-670-6 **$16.99**

The Seven Questions You're Asked in Heaven: Reviewing and Renewing Your
Life on Earth *By Dr. Ron Wolfson* 6 x 9, 176 pp, Quality PB, 978-1-58023-407-8 **$16.99**

Kabbalah / Mysticism

Walking the Path of the Jewish Mystic
How to Expand Your Awareness and Transform Your Life *By Rabbi Yoel Glick*
This unique guide to the nature of both physical and spiritual reality explores the body's energy centers, the many dimensions of the soul, the Divine nature and the unfolding relationship between the lower and the higher realms.
6 x 9, 224 pp, Quality PB, 978-1-58023-843-4 **$18.99**

Ehyeh: A Kabbalah for Tomorrow
By Rabbi Arthur Green, PhD 6 x 9, 224 pp, Quality PB, 978-1-58023-213-5 **$18.99**

The Gift of Kabbalah: Discovering the Secrets of Heaven, Renewing Your Life on Earth
By Tamar Frankiel, PhD 6 x 9, 256 pp, Quality PB, 978-1-58023-141-1 **$18.99**

Jewish Mysticism and the Spiritual Life: Classical Texts, Contemporary Reflections
Edited by Dr. Lawrence Fine, Dr. Eitan Fishbane and Rabbi Or N. Rose
6 x 9, 256 pp, Quality PB, 978-1-58023-719-2 **$18.99**

Meditation / Yoga

Increasing Wholeness: Jewish Wisdom & Guided Meditations to Strengthen & Calm Body, Heart, Mind & Spirit
By Rabbi Elie Kaplan Spitz Combines Jewish tradition, contemporary psychology and world spiritual writings with practical contemplative exercises to guide you to see the familiar in fresh new ways.
6 x 9, 208 pp, Quality PB, 978-1-58023-823-6 **$19.99**

Living the Life of Jewish Meditation: A Comprehensive Guide to Practice and Experience By Rabbi Yoel Glick
Combines the knowledge of Judaism with the spiritual practice of Yoga to lead you to an encounter with your true self. Includes nineteen different meditations.
6 x 9, 272 pp, Quality PB, 978-1-58023-802-1 **$18.99**

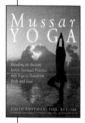

Mussar Yoga: Blending an Ancient Jewish Spiritual Practice with Yoga to Transform Body and Soul
By Edith R. Brotman, PhD, RYT-500; Foreword by Alan Morinis
A clear and easy-to-use introduction to an embodied spiritual practice for anyone seeking profound and lasting self-transformation.
7 x 9, 224 pp, 40+ b/w photos, Quality PB, 978-1-58023-784-0 **$18.99**

The Magic of Hebrew Chant: Healing the Spirit, Transforming the Mind, Deepening Love By Rabbi Shefa Gold; Foreword by Sylvia Boorstein
Introduces this transformative spiritual practice as a way to unlock the power of sacred texts and make prayer and meditation the delight of your life. Includes musical notations. 6 x 9, 352 pp, Quality PB, 978-1-58023-671-3 **$24.99**

The Magic of Hebrew Chant Companion—The Big Book of Musical Notations and Incantations 8½ x 11, 154 pp, PB, 978-1-58023-722-2 **$19.99**

Aleph-Bet Yoga: Embodying the Hebrew Letters for Physical and Spiritual Well-Being
By Steven A. Rapp; Foreword by Tamar Frankiel, PhD, and Judy Greenfeld; Preface by Hart Lazer
7 x 10, 128 pp, b/w photos, Quality PB, Lay-flat binding, 978-1-58023-162-6 **$16.95**

Discovering Jewish Meditation, 2nd Edition
Instruction & Guidance for Learning an Ancient Spiritual Practice
By Nan Fink Gefen, PhD 6 x 9, 208 pp, Quality PB, 978-1-58023-462-7 **$16.99**

The Handbook of Jewish Meditation Practices
A Guide for Enriching the Sabbath and Other Days of Your Life
By Rabbi David A. Cooper 6 x 9, 208 pp, Quality PB, 978-1-58023-102-2 **$16.95**

Jewish Meditation Practices for Everyday Life: Awakening Your Heart, Connecting with God By Rabbi Jeff Roth 6 x 9, 224 pp, Quality PB, 978-1-58023-397-2 **$18.99**

Ritual / Sacred Practices

God in Your Body: Kabbalah, Mindfulness and Embodied Spiritual Practice
By Jay Michaelson 6 x 9, 272 pp, Quality PB, 978-1-58023-304-0 **$18.99**

Jewish Ritual: A Brief Introduction for Christians
By Rabbi Kerry M. Olitzky and Rabbi Daniel Judson
5½ x 8½, 144 pp, Quality PB, 978-1-58023-210-4 **$14.99**

The Rituals & Practices of a Jewish Life: A Handbook for Personal Spiritual Renewal
Edited by Rabbi Kerry M. Olitzky and Rabbi Daniel Judson
6 x 9, 272 pp, Illus., Quality PB, 978-1-58023-169-5 **$19.99**

The Sacred Art of Lovingkindness: Preparing to Practice
By Rabbi Rami Shapiro 5½ x 8½, 176 pp, Quality PB, 978-1-59473-151-8 **$16.99***

Mystery & Detective Fiction

Criminal Kabbalah: An Intriguing Anthology of Jewish Mystery & Detective Fiction
Edited by Lawrence W. Raphael; Foreword by Laurie R. King
6 x 9, 256 pp, Quality PB, 978-1-58023-109-1 **$16.95**

Mystery Midrash: An Anthology of Jewish Mystery & Detective Fiction
Edited by Lawrence W. Raphael; Preface by Joel Siegel
6 x 9, 304 pp, Quality PB, 978-1-58023-055-1 **$16.95**

*A book from SkyLight Paths, Jewish Lights' sister imprint

Social Justice

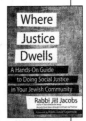

Where Justice Dwells
A Hands-On Guide to Doing Social Justice in Your Jewish Community
By Rabbi Jill Jacobs; Foreword by Rabbi David Saperstein
Provides ways to envision and act on your own ideals of social justice.
7 x 9, 288 pp, Quality PB, 978-1-58023-453-5 **$24.99**

There Shall Be No Needy
Pursuing Social Justice through Jewish Law and Tradition
By Rabbi Jill Jacobs; Foreword by Rabbi Elliot N. Dorff, PhD; Preface by Simon Greer
Confronts the most pressing issues of twenty-first-century America from a deeply Jewish perspective. 6 x 9, 288 pp, Quality PB, 978-1-58023-425-2 **$16.99**

There Shall Be No Needy Teacher's Guide 8½ x 11, 56 pp, PB, 978-1-58023-429-0 **$8.99**

Conscience
The Duty to Obey and the Duty to Disobey
By Rabbi Harold M. Schulweis (z"l)
Examines the idea of conscience and the role conscience plays in our relationships to government, law, ethics, religion, human nature, God—and to each other.
6 x 9, 160 pp, Quality PB, 978-1-58023-419-1 **$16.99**; HC, 978-1-58023-375-0 **$19.99**

Judaism and Justice: The Jewish Passion to Repair the World
By Rabbi Sidney Schwarz; Foreword by Ruth Messinger
6 x 9, 352 pp, Quality PB, 978-1-58023-353-8 **$19.99**

Spirituality / Women's Interest

Embracing the Divine Feminine: Finding God through the Ecstasy of Physical Love—The Song of Songs Annotated & Explained
Annotation and Translation by Rabbi Rami Shapiro; Foreword by Rev. Cynthia Bourgeault, PhD
Restores the Song of Songs' eroticism and interprets it as a celebration of the love between the Divine Feminine and the contemporary spiritual seeker.
5½ x 8½, 176 pp, Quality PB, 978-1-59473-575-2 **$16.99***

The Women's Haftarah Commentary
New Insights from Women Rabbis on the 54 Weekly Haftarah Portions, the 5 Megillot & Special Shabbatot
Edited by Rabbi Elyse Goldstein
Illuminates the historical significance of female portrayals in the Haftarah and the Five Megillot. 6 x 9, 560 pp, Quality PB, 978-1-58023-371-2 **$19.99**

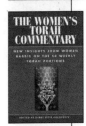

The Women's Torah Commentary
New Insights from Women Rabbis on the 54 Weekly Torah Portions
Edited by Rabbi Elyse Goldstein
Over fifty women rabbis offer inspiring insights on the Torah, in a week-by-week format.
6 x 9, 496 pp, Quality PB, 978-1-58023-370-5 **$19.99**; HC, 978-1-58023-076-6 **$34.95**

The Divine Feminine in Biblical Wisdom Literature
Selections Annotated & Explained
Translation & Annotation by Rabbi Rami Shapiro; Foreword by Rev. Cynthia Bourgeault, PhD
5½ x 8½, 240 pp, Quality PB, 978-1-59473-109-9 **$18.99***

New Jewish Feminism: Probing the Past, Forging the Future
Edited by Rabbi Elyse Goldstein; Foreword by Anita Diamant
6 x 9, 480 pp, HC, 978-1-58023-359-0 **$24.99**

The Quotable Jewish Woman
Wisdom, Inspiration & Humor from the Mind & Heart
Edited by Elaine Bernstein Partnow
6 x 9, 496 pp, Quality PB, 978-1-58023-236-4 **$19.99**

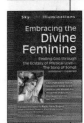

See Passover for *The Women's Passover Companion: Women's Reflections on the Festival of Freedom* and *The Women's Seder Sourcebook: Rituals & Readings for Use at the Passover Seder.*

**A book from SkyLight Paths, Jewish Lights' sister imprint*

Holidays / Holy Days

Prayers of Awe Series

An exciting new series that examines the High Holy Day liturgy to enrich the praying experience of everyone—whether experienced worshipers or guests who encounter Jewish prayer for the very first time. *Edited by Rabbi Lawrence A. Hoffman, PhD*

Who by Fire, Who by Water—*Un'taneh Tokef*
6 x 9, 272 pp, Quality PB, 978-1-58023-672-0 **$19.99**; HC, 978-1-58023-424-5 **$24.99**

All These Vows—*Kol Nidre*
6 x 9, 288 pp, HC, 978-1-58023-430-6 **$24.99**

We Have Sinned—Sin and Confession in Judaism: *Ashamnu* and *Al Chet*
6 x 9, 304 pp, HC, 978-1-58023-612-6 **$24.99**

May God Remember: Memory and Memorializing in Judaism—*Yizkor*
6 x 9, 304 pp, HC, 978-1-58023-689-8 **$24.99**

All the World: Universalism, Particularism and the High Holy Days
6 x 9, 288 pp, HC, 978-1-58023-783-3 **$24.99**

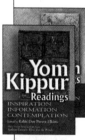

Naming God

Avinu Malkeinu—Our Father, Our King
Edited by Rabbi Lawrence A. Hoffman, PhD
Almost forty contributors from the US, Israel, UK, Europe and Canada examine one of Judaism's favorite prayers and provide analysis of the age-old but altogether modern problem of naming God. 6 x 9, 336 pp, HC, 978-1-58023-817-5 **$27.99**

Rosh Hashanah Readings: Inspiration, Information and Contemplation
Yom Kippur Readings: Inspiration, Information and Contemplation
Edited by Rabbi Dov Peretz Elkins; Section Introductions from Arthur Green's These Are the Words
Rosh Hashanah: 6 x 9, 400 pp, Quality PB, 978-1-58023-437-5 **$19.99**
Yom Kippur: 6 x 9, 368 pp, Quality PB, 978-1-58023-438-2 **$19.99**; HC, 978-1-58023-271-5 **$24.99**

Shabbat, 2nd Edition: The Family Guide to Preparing for and Celebrating the Sabbath
By Dr. Ron Wolfson 7 x 9, 320 pp, Illus., Quality PB, 978-1-58023-164-0 **$21.99**

Hanukkah, 2nd Edition: The Family Guide to Spiritual Celebration
By Dr. Ron Wolfson 7 x 9, 240 pp, Illus., Quality PB, 978-1-58023-122-0 **$18.95**

Passover

My People's Passover Haggadah

Traditional Texts, Modern Commentaries
Edited by Rabbi Lawrence A. Hoffman, PhD, and David Arnow, PhD
A diverse and exciting collection of commentaries on the traditional Passover Haggadah—in two volumes!

Vol. 1: 7 x 10, 304 pp, HC, 978-1-58023-354-5 **$24.99**
Vol. 2: 7 x 10, 320 pp, HC, 978-1-58023-346-0 **$24.99**

Creating Lively Passover Seders, 2nd Edition: A Sourcebook of Engaging Tales, Texts & Activities *By David Arnow, PhD* 7 x 9, 464 pp, Quality PB, 978-1-58023-444-3 **$24.99**

Freedom Journeys: The Tale of Exodus and Wilderness across Millennia
By Rabbi Arthur O. Waskow and Rabbi Phyllis O. Berman
6 x 9, 288 pp, HC, 978-1-58023-445-0 **$24.99**

Leading the Passover Journey: The Seder's Meaning Revealed, the Haggadah's Story Retold *By Rabbi Nathan Laufer*
6 x 9, 224 pp, Quality PB, 978-1-58023-399-6 **$18.99**

Passover, 2nd Edition: The Family Guide to Spiritual Celebration
By Dr. Ron Wolfson with Joel Lurie Grishaver 7 x 9, 416 pp, Quality PB, 978-1-58023-174-9 **$19.95**

The Women's Passover Companion: Women's Reflections on the Festival of Freedom
Edited by Rabbi Sharon Cohen Anisfeld, Tara Mohr and Catherine Spector
Foreword by Paula E. Hyman
6 x 9, 352 pp, Quality PB, 978-1-58023-231-9 **$19.99**; HC, 978-1-58023-128-2 **$24.95**

The Women's Seder Sourcebook: Rituals & Readings for Use at the Passover Seder
Edited by Rabbi Sharon Cohen Anisfeld, Tara Mohr and Catherine Spector
6 x 9, 384 pp, Quality PB, 978-1-58023-232-6 **$19.99**

Life Cycle
Marriage / Parenting / Family / Aging

Jewish Spiritual Parenting: Wisdom, Activities, Rituals and Prayers for Raising Children with Spiritual Balance and Emotional Wholeness
By Rabbi Paul Kipnes and Michelle November, MSSW
Offers parents, grandparents, teachers and anyone who interacts with children creative first steps and next steps to make the Jewish holidays and every day engaging and inspiring. 6 x 9, 224 pp, Quality PB, 978-1-58023-821-2 **$18.99**

Jewish Wisdom for Growing Older: Finding Your Grit & Grace Beyond Midlife *By Rabbi Dayle A. Friedman, MSW, MA, BCC* Mines ancient Jewish wisdom for values, tools and precedents to embrace new opportunities and beginnings, shifting family roles and experiences of illness and death.
6 x 9, 176 pp, Quality PB, 978-1-58023-819-9 **$16.99**

Ethical Wills & How to Prepare Them
A Guide to Sharing Your Values from Generation to Generation
Edited by Rabbi Jack Riemer and Dr. Nathaniel Stampfer; Foreword by Rabbi Harold S. Kushner
A unique combination of "what is" and "how to" with examples of ethical wills and a step-by-step process that shows you how to prepare your own.
6 x 9, 272 pp, Quality PB, 978-1-58023-827-4 **$18.99**

Secrets of a Soulful Marriage: Creating & Sustaining a Loving, Sacred Relationship *By Jim Sharon, EdD, and Ruth Sharon, MS*
Useful perspectives, tools and practices for cultivating a relationship; with insights from psychology, the wisdom of spiritual traditions and the experiences of many kinds of committed couples. 6 x 9, 192 pp, Quality PB, 978-1-59473-554-7 **$16.99***

Celebrating Your New Jewish Daughter: Creating Jewish Ways to Welcome Baby Girls into the Covenant—New and Traditional Ceremonies *By Debra Nussbaum Cohen Foreword by Rabbi Sandy Eisenberg Sasso* 6 x 9, 272 pp, Quality PB, 978-1-58023-090-2 **$18.95**

The Creative Jewish Wedding Book, 2nd Edition: A Hands-On Guide to New & Old Traditions, Ceremonies & Celebrations *By Gabrielle Kaplan-Mayer*
9 x 9, 288 pp, b/w photos, Quality PB, 978-1-58023-398-9 **$19.99**

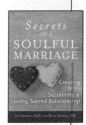

Divorce Is a Mitzvah: A Practical Guide to Finding Wholeness and Holiness When Your Marriage Dies *By Rabbi Perry Netter; Afterword by Rabbi Laura Geller*
6 x 9, 224 pp, Quality PB, 978-1-58023-172-5 **$18.99**

Embracing the Covenant: Converts to Judaism Talk About Why & How
By Rabbi Allan Berkowitz and Patti Moskovitz 6 x 9, 192 pp, Quality PB, 978-1-879045-50-7 **$18.99**

The Jewish Pregnancy Book: A Resource for the Soul, Body & Mind during Pregnancy, Birth & the First Three Months
By Sandy Falk, MD, and Rabbi Daniel Judson, with Steven A. Rapp
7 x 10, 208 pp, b/w photos, Quality PB, 978-1-58023-178-7 **$16.95**

Jewish Visions for Aging: A Professional Guide for Fostering Wholeness
By Rabbi Dale A. Friedman, MSW, MAJCS, BCC; Foreword by Thomas R. Cole, PhD
Preface by Dr. Eugene B. Borowitz 6 x 9, 272 pp, HC, 978-1-58023-348-4 **$24.99**

Making a Successful Jewish Interfaith Marriage: The Big Tent Judaism Guide to Opportunities, Challenges and Resources *By Rabbi Kerry M. Olitzky with Joan Peterson Littman*
6 x 9, 176 pp, Quality PB, 978-1-58023-170-1 **$18.99**

A Man's Responsibility: A Jewish Guide to Being a Son, a Partner in Marriage, a Father and a Community Leader *By Rabbi Joseph B. Meszler*
6 x 9, 192 pp, Quality PB, 978-1-58023-435-1 **$16.99**

The New Jewish Baby Album: Creating and Celebrating the Beginning of a Spiritual Life—A Jewish Lights Companion
By the Editors at Jewish Lights; Foreword by Anita Diamant; Preface by Rabbi Sandy Eisenberg Sasso
8 x 10, 64 pp, Deluxe Padded HC, Full-color illus., 978-1-58023-138-1 **$19.95**

The New Jewish Baby Book, 2nd Edition: Names, Ceremonies & Customs—A Guide for Today's Families *By Anita Diamant* 6 x 9, 320 pp, Quality PB, 978-1-58023-251-7 **$19.99**

Parenting Jewish Teens: A Guide for the Perplexed
By Joanne Doades 6 x 9, 176 pp, Quality PB, 978-1-58023-305-7 **$16.99**

**A book from SkyLight Paths, Jewish Lights' sister imprint*

Graphic Novels / Graphic History

The Adventures of Rabbi Harvey: A Graphic Novel of Jewish Wisdom and Wit in the Wild West *By Steve Sheinkin*
6 x 9, 144 pp, Full-color illus., Quality PB, 978-1-58023-310-1 **$16.99**

Rabbi Harvey Rides Again: A Graphic Novel of Jewish Folktales Let Loose in the Wild West *By Steve Sheinkin*
6 x 9, 144 pp, Full-color illus., Quality PB, 978-1-58023-347-7 **$16.99**

Rabbi Harvey vs. the Wisdom Kid: A Graphic Novel of Dueling Jewish Folktales in the Wild West *By Steve Sheinkin*
6 x 9, 144 pp, Full-color illus., Quality PB, 978-1-58023-422-1 **$16.99**

The Story of the Jews: A 4,000-Year Adventure—A Graphic History Book
By Stan Mack 6 x 9, 304 pp, Illus., Quality PB, 978-1-58023-155-8 **$18.99**

Ecology / Environment

A Wild Faith: Jewish Ways into Wilderness, Wilderness Ways into Judaism
By Rabbi Mike Comins; Foreword by Nigel Savage
6 x 9, 240 pp, Quality PB, 978-1-58023-316-3 **$18.99**

Ecology & the Jewish Spirit: Where Nature & the Sacred Meet
Edited by Ellen Bernstein 6 x 9, 288 pp, Quality PB, 978-1-58023-082-7 **$18.99**

Torah of the Earth: Exploring 4,000 Years of Ecology in Jewish Thought
Vol. 1: Biblical Israel & Rabbinic Judaism; Vol. 2: Zionism & Eco-Judaism
Edited by Rabbi Arthur Waskow Vol. 1: 6 x 9, 272 pp, Quality PB, 978-1-58023-086-5 **$19.95**
Vol. 2: 6 x 9, 336 pp, Quality PB, 978-1-58023-087-2 **$19.95**

The Way Into Judaism and the Environment *By Jeremy Benstein, PhD*
6 x 9, 288 pp, Quality PB, 978-1-58023-368-2 **$18.99**; HC, 978-1-58023-268-5 **$24.99**

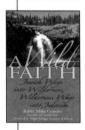

Grief / Healing

Facing Illness, Finding God: How Judaism Can Help You and Caregivers Cope
When Body or Spirit Fails *By Rabbi Joseph B. Meszler*
6 x 9, 208 pp, Quality PB, 978-1-58023-423-8 **$16.99**

Grief in Our Seasons: A Mourner's Kaddish Companion *By Rabbi Kerry M. Olitzky*
4½ x 6½, 448 pp, Quality PB, 978-1-879045-55-2 **$18.99**

Healing and the Jewish Imagination: Spiritual and Practical Perspectives on
Judaism and Health *Edited by Rabbi William Cutter, PhD*
6 x 9, 240 pp, Quality PB, 978-1-58023-373-6 **$19.99**

Healing from Despair: Choosing Wholeness in a Broken World
By Rabbi Elie Kaplan Spitz with Erica Shapiro Taylor; Foreword by Abraham J. Twerski, MD
5½ x 8½, 208 pp, Quality PB, 978-1-58023-436-8 **$16.99**

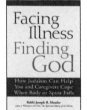

Healing of Soul, Healing of Body: Spiritual Leaders Unfold the Strength & Solace
in Psalms *Edited by Rabbi Simkha Y. Weintraub, LCSW*
6 x 9, 128 pp, 2-color illus. text, Quality PB, 978-1-879045-31-6 **$16.99**

Judaism and Health: A Handbook of Practical, Professional and Scholarly Resources
Edited by Jeff Levin, PhD, MPH, and Michele F. Prince, LCSW, MAJCS
Foreword by Rabbi Elliot N. Dorff, PhD 6 x 9, 448 pp, HC, 978-1-58023-714-7 **$50.00**

Midrash & Medicine: Healing Body and Soul in the Jewish Interpretive Tradition
Edited by Rabbi William Cutter, PhD; Foreword by Michele F. Prince, LCSW, MAJCS
6 x 9, 352 pp, Quality PB, 978-1-58023-484-9 **$21.99**

Mourning & Mitzvah, 2nd Edition: A Guided Journal for Walking the Mourner's
Path through Grief to Healing *By Rabbi Anne Brener, LCSW*
7½ x 9, 304 pp, Quality PB, 978-1-58023-113-8 **$19.99**

Tears of Sorrow, Seeds of Hope, 2nd Edition: A Jewish Spiritual Companion
for Infertility and Pregnancy Loss *By Rabbi Nina Beth Cardin*
6 x 9, 208 pp, Quality PB, 978-1-58023-233-3 **$18.99**

A Time to Mourn, a Time to Comfort, 2nd Edition
A Guide to Jewish Bereavement *By Dr. Ron Wolfson; Foreword by Rabbi David J. Wolpe*
7 x 9, 384 pp, Quality PB, 978-1-58023-253-1 **$21.99**

When a Grandparent Dies: A Kid's Own Remembering Workbook for Dealing
with Shiva and the Year Beyond *By Nechama Liss-Levinson, PhD*
8 x 10, 48 pp, 2-color text, HC, 978-1-879045-44-6 **$15.95** *For ages 7–13*

Bar / Bat Mitzvah

The Mitzvah Project Book
Making Mitzvah Part of Your Bar/Bat Mitzvah ... and Your Life
By Liz Suneby and Diane Heiman; Foreword by Rabbi Jeffrey K. Salkin; Preface by Rabbi Sharon Brous
The go-to source for Jewish young adults and their families looking to make the
world a better place through good deeds—big or small.
6 x 9, 224 pp, Quality PB, 978-1-58023-458-0 **$16.99** *For ages 11–13*
     Workshop Leader's Guide: 8½ x 11, 9 pp, PB, 978-1-58023-530-3 **$8.99**

The Bar/Bat Mitzvah Memory Book, 2nd Edition: An Album for Treasuring
the Spiritual Celebration *By Rabbi Jeffrey K. Salkin and Nina Salkin*
8 x 10, 48 pp, 2-color text, Deluxe HC, ribbon marker, 978-1-58023-263-0 **$19.99**

For Kids—Putting God on Your Guest List, 2nd Edition: How to Claim the
Spiritual Meaning of Your Bar or Bat Mitzvah *By Rabbi Jeffrey K. Salkin*
6 x 9, 144 pp, Quality PB, 978-1-58023-308-8 **$16.99** *For ages 11–13*

The Jewish Prophet: Visionary Words from Moses and Miriam to Henrietta Szold
and A. J. Heschel *By Rabbi Dr. Michael J. Shire*
6½ x 8½, 128 pp, 123 full-color illus., HC, 978-1-58023-168-8 **$14.95**

Putting God on the Guest List, 3rd Edition: How to Reclaim the Spiritual
Meaning of Your Child's Bar or Bat Mitzvah *By Rabbi Jeffrey K. Salkin*
6 x 9, 224 pp, Quality PB, 978-1-58023-222-7 **$18.99**
     Teacher's Guide: 8½ x 11, 48 pp, PB, 978-1-58023-226-5 **$8.99**

Teens / Young Adults

Text Messages: A Torah Commentary for Teens
Edited by Rabbi Jeffrey K. Salkin
Shows today's teens how each Torah portion contains worlds of meaning for
them, for what they are going through in their lives, and how they can shape their
Jewish identity as they enter adulthood.
6 x 9, 304 pp, HC, 978-1-58023-507-5 **$24.99**

Hannah Senesh: Her Life and Diary, the First Complete Edition
By Hannah Senesh; Foreword by Marge Piercy; Preface by Eitan Senesh; Afterword by Roberta Grossman
6 x 9, 368 pp, b/w photos, Quality PB, 978-1-58023-342-2 **$19.99**

I Am Jewish: Personal Reflections Inspired by the Last Words of Daniel Pearl
Edited by Judea and Ruth Pearl 6 x 9, 304 pp, Deluxe PB w/ flaps, 978-1-58023-259-3 **$19.99**
Download a free copy of the *I Am Jewish Teacher's Guide* at www.jewishlights.com.

The JGirl's Guide: The Young Jewish Woman's Handbook for Coming of Age
By Penina Adelman, Ali Feldman and Dr. Shulamit Reinharz
6 x 9, 240 pp, Quality PB, 978-1-58023-215-9 **$16.99** *For ages 11 & up*
     Teacher's & Parent's Guide: 8½ x 11, 56 pp, PB, 978-1-58023-225-8 **$8.99**

The JGuy's Guide: The GPS for Jewish Teen Guys
By Rabbi Joseph B. Meszler, Dr. Shulamit Reinharz, Liz Suneby and Diane Heiman
6 x 9, 208 pp, Quality PB, 978-1-58023-721-5 **$16.99**
     Teacher's Guide: 8½ x 11, 30 pp, PB, 978-1-58023-773-4 **$8.99**

Tough Questions Jews Ask, 2nd Edition: A Young Adult's Guide to Building a
Jewish Life *By Rabbi Edward Feinstein*
6 x 9, 160 pp, Quality PB, 978-1-58023-454-2 **$16.99** *For ages 11 & up*
     Teacher's Guide: 8½ x 11, 72 pp, PB, 978-1-58023-187-9 **$8.95**

Pre-Teens

Be Like God: God's To-Do List for Kids
By Dr. Ron Wolfson
Encourages kids ages eight through twelve to use their God-given superpowers
to find the many ways they can make a difference in the lives of others and find
meaning and purpose for their own.
7 x 9, 144 pp, Quality PB, 978-1-58023-510-5 **$15.99** *For ages 8–12*

The Book of Miracles: A Young Person's Guide to Jewish Spiritual Awareness
By Lawrence Kushner, with all-new illustrations by the author
6 x 9, 96 pp, 2-color illus., HC, 978-1-879045-78-1 **$16.95** *For ages 9–13*

About Jewish Lights

People of all faiths and backgrounds yearn for books that attract, engage, educate, and spiritually inspire.

Our principal goal is to stimulate thought and help all people learn about who the Jewish People are, where they come from, and what the future can be made to hold. While people of our diverse Jewish heritage are the primary audience, our books speak to people in the Christian world as well and will broaden their understanding of Judaism and the roots of their own faith.

We bring to you authors who are at the forefront of spiritual thought and experience. While each has something different to say, they all say it in a voice that you can hear.

Our books are designed to welcome you and then to engage, stimulate, and inspire. We judge our success not only by whether or not our books are beautiful and commercially successful, but by whether or not they make a difference in your life.

For your information and convenience, at the back of this book we have provided a list of other Jewish Lights books you might find interesting and useful. They cover all the categories of your life:

Bar/Bat Mitzvah	Life Cycle
Bible Study / Midrash	Meditation
Children's Books	Men's Interest
Congregation Resources	Parenting
Current Events / History	Prayer / Ritual / Sacred Practice
Ecology / Environment	Social Justice
Fiction: Mystery, Science Fiction	Spirituality
Grief / Healing	Theology / Philosophy
Holidays / Holy Days	Travel
Inspiration	Twelve Steps
Kabbalah / Mysticism / Enneagram	Women's Interest

JEWISH LIGHTS is an imprint of

TURNER
PUBLISHING COMPANY